Selecting and Using Training Aids

PRACTICAL TRAINER SERIES

Selecting and Using Training Aids

DAVID FLEGG   JOSEPHINE McHALE

Pfeiffer
& COMPANY

San Diego • Toronto • Amsterdam • Sydney

Acorn, Archimedes, Apple Macintosh, Atari ST, Barco, BBC Enterprises, BBC Micro, Commodore, Amiga, Flipframe, Grundig, Hypercard, HyperTalk, IBM AT, IBM PC, Linkway, Longman Training, Macintosh II, MIC, PC Opensoft, Designsoft, Presentsoft, Searchsoft, Phillips, PS/2, TenCore are all trademarks or registered names of their respective organizations.

First published in 1991 by Kogan Page, in association with the Institute of Training and Development.

Kogan Page Limited
120 Pentonville Road
London N1 9JN

© David Flegg and Josephine McHale, 1991

Published in the United States of America by
 Pfeiffer & Company
 8517 Production Avenue
 San Diego, CA 92121-2280
 (619) 578-5900
 FAX (619) 578-2042

British Library Cataloguing in Publication Data

A CIP record for this book is available from the British Library.

ISBN   0 7494 0412 4

This book is printed on acid-free, recycled stock that meets or exceeds the
minimum GPO and EPA specifications for recycled paper.

Contents

Acknowledgements

We offer our sincere thanks to the following organizations, who have given their kind permission to reproduce photographs and stills of their products.

Barco (UK) Ltd
Enterprise PR
Folex Film Systems
MAR-COM Group plc
Longman Training.

We would also like to thank the following, who have supplied us with information about many of the training aids we describe in the book.

Association of Professional Video Distributors
Audio Visual, Video and Presentation Advisory Service
Don Gresswell Limited
Edric Audio Visual Ltd
Elite Optics Limited
Folex Film Systems
Hanimex (UK) Ltd
Harpers AV Limited
Kodak Limited
Polaroid (UK) Ltd
Rediffusion Simulation Ltd
The Saville Group Limited

The Soft Option
Sony (UK) Ltd
Staedtler (UK) Ltd
TWS plc
David Welham, Group Manager ITS, Rediffusion Simulation Ltd

Series Editor's Foreword

Organizations get things done when people do their jobs effectively. To make this happen they need to be well trained. A number of people are likely to be involved in this training by identifying the needs of the organization and of the individual, by selecting or designing appropriate training to meet those needs, by delivering it and by assessing how effective it was. It is not only 'professional' or full-time trainers who are involved in this process: personnel managers, line managers, supervisors and job holders are all likely to have a part to play.

This series has been written for all those who get involved with training in some way or another, whether they are senior personnel managers trying to link the goals of the organization with training needs or job holders who have been given responsibility for training newcomers. Therefore, the series is essentially a practical one which focuses on specific aspects of the training function. This is not to say that the theoretical underpinnings of the practical aspects of training are unimportant. Anyone seriously interested in training is strongly encouraged to look beyond 'what to do' and 'how to do it' and to delve into the areas of why things are done in a particular way.

The authors have been selected because they have considerable practical experience. All have shared, at some time, the same difficulties, frustrations and satisfactions of being involved in training and are now in a position to share with others some helpful and practical guidelines.

In this book David Flegg and Josephine McHale discuss the selection and use of training aids; a term which to many of us is synonymous with visual aids and is usually the final stage of our preparation. However, it can be seen that there are close links with training objectives that should make the selection of training aids an integral part of our planning. Once it has been established what trainees will be expected to do at the end of training, the trainer must consider what aids to their learning will best help them to be able to do it. This extends the concept of training aids beyond visual aids to include role-play, case studies, simulation and other strategies which support the learning process.

ROGER BUCKLEY

Preface

If you look at suppliers' catalogues of training aids, you'll see the trainer cast as the central player in an electronic orchestra. Armed with a laser pointer and various remote control devices, you press a button and the projection screen unfurls from its ceiling mounting; press another button and the whiteboard emerges noiselessly from behind its camouflage panels; you cue the computer presentation system, and begin to speak. The audience sits expectantly.

To the seasoned performer, whose speciality is slick, professional presentations, maybe this sounds like the basic necessities of the trade. If you are addressing a major international conference, or compering a PR event, maybe nothing less will do. To the trainer, whose job is to help people learn, it probably sounds like a technological nightmare: so many things could go wrong.

This takes us back to the equipment catalogues: in their sections on training aids, they are in fact describing *presentation* aids. They beguile you with enticing descriptions of whiteboards that will give you a photocopy of everything you have written (What? All that scribble?); printers that print A1 sheets (very impressive, but handwriting will do); a palette that turns your humble overhead projector into a computer slide presentation system (a shame you haven't got time to get to grips with that graphics package); and yes, you can still buy a box of transparencies and a pad of flipchart paper.

But this is all about *giving* information, which is only one aspect of the trainer's job. Training should be about helping people to learn – to think, question, apply, analyse and understand. Training aids are not just a means of getting a message across: they are anything (with the emphasis on *thing* – we're not talking about *methods* of training) that you can use to enhance your training in all its subtlety and complexity.

Aims of this Book

This book has been written to:

- help you make rational decisions about using training aids. We discuss the all-important training related criteria and also bring into the open the other criteria, such as familiarity and convenience, that often take precedence.
- offer you a short-cut to success. Each training aid has its own set of pitfalls that trap the unwary. By alerting you to these, we can save you the painful process of having to learn in public from your mistakes.
- give you confidence – the confidence of knowing that you are using training aids effectively and appropriately.

Is this Book for You?

If you are relatively new to the training function, then you may still be finding your way around the various training aids and learning how to use them effectively. If so, you should find this book a useful starting point. Alternatively, you may be a more experienced trainer, but anxious not to get stuck in a rut. In this case, you should find the guidance given on using training aids a useful way of checking your performance, and whether or not you are exploiting the aids to the full.

But you don't need to be a trainer to benefit from this book. You may be a manager involved in a 'cascade' process, disseminating information throughout a department, or with a responsibility for holding regular briefing meetings, or running group discussion and brainstorming sessions. In these circumstances, you may not see yourself as a trainer, but the methods and skills you will use will overlap. It follows, then, that you will need the so-called 'training aids'.

Technology features strongly in this book. This is not because we recommend moving towards the more technical end of the spectrum when you choose your training aids; on the contrary, our advice would be to err on the side of simplicity. However, you should know what equipment is available and how to use it to its full advantage, so that you can make an informed choice about what would best suit your needs in particular circumstances.

How this Book is Organized

Part 1: Selecting Training Aids

- Chapter 1 is concerned with why you might want to use training aids at all. Once you've decided that you do need some form of training aid, we offer some criteria for choosing appropriately.
- Chapter 2 is about how you can use training aids to create the right conditions for people to learn. Different aids are often associated with different training methods.
- Chapter 3 lists the most common training methods. For each one, there's a description of its main purpose, its characteristics and the training aids most likely to be used.

Part 2: Using Training Aids

This second part of the book describes in detail the various training aids you are likely to encounter. Where appropriate, a convention of dealing with each type under a series of headings has been adopted. These cover:

- a description of the equipment
- the main training applications
- any preparation that is needed (e.g. setting up equipment)
- a guide to producing materials (e.g. OHP transparencies)
- some tips on good training practice.

In Chapters 8–10, this convention is not used because of the sheer variety of examples.

How to use this Book

How you use this book will depend on what you want to get out of it. Taken as a whole, it provides a progressively more detailed account of where training aids might be used and how to use them for greatest effect, but it's unlikely that you'll want to read the book from cover to cover. If you want to be systematic, and set things in context, then we suggest that you read Chapters 1–3 in their entirety and then dip into Chapters 4 to 10 as the need arises. But if you haven't got time to do this, *Selecting and Using Training Aids* can be used as a valuable reference source.

Part 1 Selecting Training Aids

1 Criteria for Choosing Training Aids

▷ SUMMARY ◁

This chapter:
- Outlines a three-stage process to planning training courses.
- Relates decisions about choice of training aids to the planning stages.
- Offers criteria for making the decisions.

Why do trainers use training aids? To make their training more effective, of course. Put the question slightly differently, though, and ask: 'Why do trainers use certain training aids rather than others?', and the answers will be altogether more interesting, and not necessarily related to the nature of the training.

In this chapter, we look at the criteria used in choosing training aids and put them into a coherent framework.

The Starting Point

If you read Robert Mager's classic text *Preparing Instructional Objectives*, you will find that a well-formulated objective includes three things:

- what a learner is expected to *do*
- the important conditions under which the performance is to occur
- the standards of performance that will be considered acceptable.

Most trainers at least pay lip service to this, but what, you might be asking, has objective-setting got to do with choosing training aids? The link, in fact, is very close. What you want people to be able to do as a result of your training will determine the training methods that you will use. The methods will then determine and be complemented by your choice of training aids. The extent to which they make your training more effective depends on how accurately you defined the expected outcomes in the first place.

Put like this, it sounds a very short step between objectives and training aids. For training events run to a well-tried formula, this may indeed be true. It might also be perfectly acceptable. On the other hand, it could mean that accepted practice is never challenged, and that decisions are made on the basis of outdated assumptions or expediency. It's useful to step back occasionally and take a more strategic view.

Strategic Planning

Imagine that you've done a thorough analysis of training needs and are now ready to begin planning the actual training programme. Where do you begin? If you have accepted the need to think strategically and systematically, then you have already found the right place to start. The planning itself can be divided into three sequential stages.

Stage 1:

At this stage, you need to be defining:

- what you are trying to achieve
- what, if any, constraints you will have to work under
- what sort of media and training methods would be appropriate to the subject matter.

'What you are trying to achieve' means specifying your objectives, and making them as performance-related as possible, but this isn't something that can be done in isolation. To be realistic, you will have to take into account certain practical constraints, such as:

- how much time your target audience can spare for a training course
- how accessible the audience is
- how many trainers could be made available
- what resources you could draw on

 − the size of your budget
 − the timescale over which the training has to be designed and delivered.

Moving from your objectives to choosing media and methods is again a question of starting with what you would like to do and then reconsidering it in the light of reality. The fundamental question must be: 'What sort of experience will people need in order to achieve the objectives?' At its most basic, this means deciding which channels of communication need to be involved. The five senses of sight, sound, touch, taste, smell are self-explanatory. The sixth sense − the kinaesthetic sense − is less so. It refers to the sensory channel that tells us when our muscles are doing what they should be doing in the right way. For example, before the advent of electronic keyboards, novice typists had to learn to type with an even pressure on each finger in order to get a consistent imprint on the paper: they had to develop a kinaesthetic sense.

The majority of training situations require trainees to use just the senses of sight and sound. There are times when either would be suitable; for example, certain information might be just as easily assimilated by listening or reading.

For most office-based personnel, it is realistic to concentrate on this narrow range of senses. The occasions when these trainees would need to rely on their sense of taste, smell, touch or kinaesthesia will be very limited. These other senses come into their own in the more practical and physical arenas such as catering, engineering, driving/flying or practising medicine. For example, a chef feels as well as sees when dough is sufficiently mixed; a doctor diagnoses through touch as well as sight and sound; anyone proficient in the use of tools will get a satisfying kinaesthetic feeling of 'rightness' from applying their skills.

Your first decision in planning your training, then, is whether the nature of the task demands that a particular sense must be involved. You must then decide whether involving more than one sense, although not strictly necessary, would be helpful. For example, young children initially learn language purely by listening to people; some language teachers might use this as a justification for teaching adults a second language in the same way − using just the auditory sense. However, for most people, the combination of listening and seeing the words written down would be more effective − involving the extra sense improves their retention.

Deciding on which senses have to be used leads naturally on to choosing the training method. For example, kinaesthetic feedback

19

comes only from hands-on experience, either of the real thing or of a simulated version; if learners need to see something, then you must incorporate some sort of visual presentation.

Another dimension needs to be taken account of at this stage. Merely listening or watching, or even both together, can leave learners in a *passive* receiver state. Their learning will be more effective if they can switch to an active processing mode. And so you must decide on those training methods that will involve participants in thinking, discriminating, analysing, comparing – in fact, in whatever mental processes are appropriate to your training objectives. At this point, you might float away in clouds of fantasy, designing the ultimate training event. You come down to earth abruptly, though, when you realize that your choice of training methods is subject to the same sort of constraints as applied to decisions about what your training should try to achieve. You are limited by the access to your target audience and the resources you can draw on.

Once you have made your decision about *methods*, you are ready to consider how to complement them with some well-chosen training *aids*. At this point time plays a major part in your plans. If your course is due to run for the first time two weeks hence, you don't start scripting a video or investigating computer projection systems and their associated graphics packages. You might pencil in these options for the future if your course has a long shelf-life, but in the short-term, you will have to be more modest in your choices.

Stage 2

At this stage, you will begin to translate your strategic decisions into a more detailed plan. In terms of the design of your course, it means deciding on the:

- detailed objectives
- sequence of events
- content to be covered.

As far as methods are concerned, you will choose from the options identified in Stage 1. Your decisions about which training aids to use will depend on:

- the cost and time needed (see Figure 1.1)
- the flexibility of the equipment
- the characteristics of your target audience.

Cost is a complicated criterion to sort out. You will need to consider whether:

— a large initial investment (e.g. hardware and software for producing graphics, plus the time needed to learn how to use the package) might be an economy in the longer term (by saving you the time and money needed for using a design studio)

Training aid	Relative cost and time to prepare		
	Equipment cost	Materials cost	Time to prepare materials
Whiteboards/ flipcharts etc	low	v. low	short
OHP/slides	med	low	short - med
Audio tapes	low	low - med	short - med
Video (pre- recorded)	med	low - high	med
Video (CCTV)	med - high	low	short
Video (comm- issioned prog)	n/a	v. high	med - long
Job aids	low - med	low - med	short - med
Handouts	v. low	low	short
Simulator	low - v. high	low - v. high	short - long
Computer	med - high	low - high	med - long

Basis for categories

Cost
low: less than £500
med: £500 - £2,000
high: £2,000 or more

Time
short: 1 day or less
med: several days - a few weeks
long: several weeks or months

Figure 1.1 *Comparison of costs and production times for training aids*

– a more expensive option can be justified in terms of its greater effectiveness

– technical back-up would be needed (e.g. to set up and maintain equipment and for fault-finding on it if it goes wrong)

Flexibility raises issues such as:

– how easy it would be to update the output of your training aid
– how transportable and robust the training aid is.

The characteristics of your target audience that will influence your choice will include:

– the size of the total population your audience comes from
– the size of groups that you will have on a training event
– where they will be and how you will reach them (if you have to travel to them, you might think twice about carrying an interactive video workstation around with you).

Stage 3

Here the objectives need to be grouped together and translated into individual session plans, so that the course/programme develops a detailed structure.

If the appropriate decisions have been made at the previous levels, then the decisions at Stage 3 relate to the selection of *specific* materials. This means answering questions such as:

– Are suitable materials available off the shelf, or will they have to be specially made?
– Is it possible to adapt existing material?
– Is it feasible to collect 'in-house' case study material? (For example, if you want course members to analyse the way phone calls are handled, it would be easy to monitor incoming calls and to get a range of examples; the drawback is the time it would take to listen to the examples and to select the most appropriate ones.)

TRAINER'S TIP

Don't reinvent the wheel. If someone else has done something that you can use, use it.

Time scale

The three stages of strategic planning for making decisions about your training courses may sound like a protracted process. In fact, if you are designing short training events, many of the decisions can be made very quickly, provided you have got access to the right information. Longer and more complex courses will, of course, take proportionally longer to plan and decide.

Your Criteria

The process outlined so far is a very logical one in which your choice of training aids depends on earlier decisions about which methods would be appropriate, which in turn have been made as a result of the training objectives. If you accept the logic and rationale of this, then your decisions will be based on training related matters, such as:

- what you want learners to do (for example retain information; develop discrimination; improve understanding; change attitudes)
- which channels of communication/sensory stimuli therefore are necessary and which additional ones would be helpful
- creating conditions that will help people learn.

It is unrealistic to expect that decisions can be made entirely on these grounds, though. Inevitably, you will have to be realistic and work within the constraints of time, budget, and your target population, as already discussed. But this still leaves out perhaps the most powerful influence of all. When the final decisions have to be made, the deciding factor will be what you are comfortable with. It is a long way from the rational process with which this chapter started.

TRAINER'S TIP

Make a point of reviewing your training sessions, both the content and the training aids you use. Your training will grow stale if you let yourself get into a rut. Reassess your criteria regularly. The underlying assumptions might change.

---

2 Training Aids or Learning Aids?

> ## SUMMARY ◁

This chapter:
- Explains the importance of getting the active participation of trainees.
- Describes the training techniques that will encourage the above and help people learn.
- Identifies training aids that will complement the techniques.

The Trainer's Role

The trainer's role is to help people learn. Obvious? Maybe, but what does it mean in practice? The Preface mentioned that equipment catalogues give the impression that training aids are, in fact, just aids to presentation. In this context, helping people learn would mean presenting information more effectively.

If you take a broader view of learning, you will want to develop a more collaborative relationship with the participants on your courses. Far from seeing yourself as the prime source of knowledge and expertise, you will encourage them to be responsible for their own learning, and to use you and their peers as resources. If you go along with this, you will implicitly substitute the words *learning aid* for training aid, and use anything that encourages the learner to participate actively in the learning process. This doesn't exclude presentation aids, but it does cast the net more widely.

Encouraging active participation means creating the right conditions in which people feel willing and able to learn. In practice, this could mean anything from the joining instructions to the lunch menu. This chapter outlines the key conditions that can be reinforced by training aids of one sort or another. Much of the information is covered in more detail under the heading of 'Training Applications' in the later chapters on specific training aids. The emboldened words here will show what aids are explained in more detail later.

How the Trainer can Create Good Training Conditions

Level

Your course members will soon switch off if they feel the content of the course is not pitched at the right level for them. If you are running an open course, or for some other reason haven't been able to screen people in advance, then discussions and preliminary practical sessions might give you the information you need. Alternatively, where you need to assess more accurately the level of knowledge, you might find it useful to give an informal **quiz**.

Direction

Most people learn more effectively when they can see the wider picture – where they are at any particular time, where they're going next, and how it relates to where they've come from. Your course timetable and introductory remarks will provide some of this overview, but you need to build in regular signposts. You can do this effectively in the context of any inputs you might make, or in the introduction to activities, using the **OHP** or **flipchart** to record the key points.

Getting participants to complete **action plans** will help them to plot their own way forward.

Acceptance

No one is at their most receptive when they feel nervous or uncomfortable. An important part of the trainer's role is to create supportive conditions in which participants can relax and concentrate on learning.

There are several ways of doing this. The first is to explain clearly at each stage what it is that you expect people to do. Your briefing notes and use of the **OHP** or **flipchart** will be helpful here.

The second consideration is to minimize the threat associated with performing in front of other people. This is partly a question of using your skills to prepare participants for particular activities (such as role-playing in front of the video camera), but it can also be a matter of how you have written the **handouts** in which the activities themselves are described. The easier it is to extract the relevant information, the more the individual can concentrate on what really matters.

Recognition

Each of us likes to be treated as an individual, and to be recognized for what we can contribute. Using the **flipchart** and **OHP** to note what individuals have said can be a powerful way of maintaining their attention and involvement.

Clarity of presentation

Training is much more than a series of presentations, but where you do have information to impart it should be presented as clearly and helpfully as possible. The **OHP** and **flipchart** are both excellent for displaying key points, summaries, etc. If you need to show more complex diagrams or pictures of real objects, then one of the **projection methods** will be invaluable.

Reducing the memory load

Putting into practice recently learned knowledge and/or skills can impose a considerable memory load. If it is more important to practise and get feedback on other parts of a task, rather than to demonstrate that information has been memorized accurately, then various **job aids** can reduce the strain.

Active involvement

If you include presentations in your training courses and ask only that people watch and listen, then you have no real indication of how much they are concentrating. You can be fairly sure, though, that their attention will oscillate between you, the view from the window, other participants, what's going on at work, what will happen that evening . . . With the best will in the world, it's difficult to concentrate undividedly on a speaker for more than a few minutes at a time.

The situation changes dramatically if you give your audience something to do. This does not mean throwing out a token question every now and again. It means preparing **interactive handouts** that require mental activity at regular intervals, and help to keep your audience interested and attentive.

Simulating reality

At the end of a training course, each participant will go back to work and face the challenge of applying what has been learned. You will no doubt have tried to create activities and experiences that incorporate the essential features of reality, so that transferring from the course to work goes as smoothly as possible. In the context of developing behavioural skills, the **video recorder** provides a valuable back-up to the semi-real situations that have been created in role-plays. Faced with an indisputable record of what has happened, even the most resistant participant will learn something.

Individual responsibility

You cannot make another person learn; you can only do your utmost to create conditions in which it is easy for people to learn. Having done as much as you can, encourage them to take over the responsibility, by reviewing their own progress and planning their next steps. Well designed **self-assessment sheets** and **action plans** are invaluable aids to learning.

TRAINER'S TIP

Keep asking yourself the fundamental question: 'How can I help people learn more effectively?' Consider every training aid from the trainee's point of view.

3 Matching the Training Aid to the Training Method

▷   SUMMARY   ◁

This chapter:
- Summarises the key training methods, their usefulness and their characteristics
- Identifies the training aids appropriate to each method

At Stage 3 of the planning process outlined in Chapter 1, the detailed structure of individual sessions begins to emerge. This is the point at which you choose your training method and select the most suitable training aids to complement it, bearing in mind all the constraints of time, cost, ease of production etc.

In this chapter, the most common training methods are briefly discussed in terms of what they can most successfully be used for together with some characteristics that are worth bearing in mind when deciding how to use them. For each method, the training aids that would be appropriate are listed and they are summarized in Figure 3.1 at the end of the chapter.

Training Methods

Presentations

Presentations are most useful for putting across *information*, particularly to a large audience. A sufficiently persuasive and skillful presenter could have a large impact on the audience's attitudes.

Characteristics

Most presenters stand in front of their audience and talk at them, supplementing what they say with visual aids. Interaction with the audience tends to be on a formal basis ('I'll take questions at the end, please'). The impact depends both on the presenter's skill as a speaker and on the imagination with which the visuals were designed. Smaller groups, such as those found on most training courses, tend to soften the formality of a presentation, either because someone interrupts with a question well before the end, or because the presenter/trainer deliberately breaks up the flow by involving the audience.

Associated training aids

It is hard to listen for more than a few minutes at a time, which is why presenters like to give the audience something to look at as well. If you need to make a presentation, you might consider backing up your speech with:

- OHP transparencies
- flipchart displays (mainly for informal situations)
- slides (particularly for formal presentations)
- interactive handouts for those times when you want to involve your audience and to maintain interest
- handouts to provide a record of the content for individuals' future reference
- other sources of audio or visual material, such as excerpts from audio or video tapes, or projections of original documents, three dimensional objects etc.

Group Discussion

'Group discussion' is a catch-all category that covers a multitude of uses. At one extreme, it can degenerate into an ill-defined activity that is allowed to occur when the trainer has run out of ideas for anything more constructive. On the other hand, it can be used in a structured way for very specific purposes, such as to:

- break the ice at the beginning of a course, to find out where people are starting from, and to set the agenda for the rest of the course
- explore attitudes
- solve problems
- explore applications of what has been learned
- analyse the implications of a training video, or other activity

– plan (for an immediate activity or for something longer term)
– simulate work-related discussions, and provide realistic data for subsequent analysis of the process.

Characteristics
Group discussions tend to be loosely structured and go off in directions unforeseen by the trainer. You should make clear to every participant, the purpose and expected outcomes of a discussion group.

Associated training aids
Because of the unpredictability of discussion groups, training aids are introduced to give some structure and focus. Handouts will be used to provide:

– information on the purpose of the discussion
– any necessary background information – somewhere for participants to make notes and record outcomes.

Key points of the discussion might usefully be recorded on a flipchart, and later displayed around the room for reference and analysis. An OHP or whiteboard could be used instead, but are less easy to refer to later.

Demonstrations

A demonstration is a more flexible method of training than might at first appear. It can be used to show part or all of a procedure or skill, and as a positive model, or as a warning of what not to do. The skillful demonstrator will avoid overloading learners by knowing when to offer them the chance to practise for themselves. For example, an experienced bricklayer might begin to teach a group of novices by demonstrating the whole procedure from picking up the cement with a trowel, applying it to the brick, settling the brick in the appropriate position and checking that it was level. Next would come a demonstration of the component skills, each followed by individual practice by every trainee.

Characteristics
To learn from a demonstration, each learner should have a clear view of what they are being shown and the opportunity to practise the procedure or skill either in parts or as a whole.

Associated training aids
The demonstrator's major training aid is the equipment or tools used for the demonstration. However, giving each learner a clear view of what is being demonstrated isn't always easy, particularly if certain

parts of the equipment can be located only by feel. The trainer might decide to work on a one-to-one basis, or with very small groups, so that each person can see and touch whatever is necessary. Alternatively, in some cases, it might be feasible to increase visibility with training aids, by:

- showing a good quality video of the whole process on a large screen
- projecting on to a screen a large diagram or photograph of what is difficult to see in actuality
- using a video projector to show a demonstration on small pieces of equipment
- displaying a clear diagram on the OHP or flipchart.

There are further complications with visibility in relation to physical skills when the action happens so quickly that it's impossible to see what is involved. In this case, a useful training aid would be a video recording, showing the actions in slow motion.

In order to give adequate practice, the trainer must either be working with small groups so that each has a turn on the demonstration equipment, or else must provide training aids in the form of real equipment, or something sufficiently like it to provide the right sort of experience. Many novice dinghy helms will watch their instructors giving a real demonstration on the water of how to tack (a common manoeuvre in sailing), and then practise the skills on dry land, with a mock-up of the boat consisting of two chairs, a piece of rope and a tiller.

Role-play Exercises

Role-play exercises offer an opportunity for practising interpersonal skills in a safe environment. Typically, participants explore ways of handling awkward situations and experiment with different ways of behaving. The exercises are particularly useful for investigating likely consequences ('What happens if I say ...?') or to explore feelings ('How does it feel to be treated this way? What's it like being on the receiving end of . . ?').

Characteristics
Role-play exercises vary from the totally spontaneous to the carefully planned and scripted. They are most effective when they're based on incidents that participants are familiar with in their work (e.g. dealing with an angry customer on the phone) or outside work (e.g. making an assertive complaint about poor service).

The background to the scenario may be provided by the trainer, or else worked out by the participants themselves.

Associated training aids

Since few participants are accomplished actors with a talent for improvisation, some degree of preparation is helpful. A useful training aid is therefore a *briefing sheet* that will provide sufficient information to help each party to play a convincing role. In some cases, both 'actors' will be given the same sheet. In others, they would have a briefing sheet appropriate to the role they are playing. (See Figure 9.1 in Chapter 9 for the 'Estate Agent's Brief' in a role-play involving negotiations between an estate agent and a potential client.)

Most activities involving interpersonal skills need little, if anything, in the way of equipment for the participants.

In terms of hardware for the trainer, video recording equipment will give you the means of recording the activity and playing it back later for analysis and discussion. Where a role-play simulates a telephone conversation, or for some other reason you want participants to rely only on what they hear rather than what they see, then use an audio cassette recorder to record just the sound.

A flipchart might be handy too, in case you want to summarize some important points for the benefit of the whole group.

Simulations

'Simulation' covers an enormous range of training situations from the simple role-play activities mentioned above, to the complexities of dealing with emergencies on an oil rig or flying an aeroplane. Similarly, the degree of fidelity varies, too. The chairs, rope and tiller mentioned previously are sufficient for the basic co-ordination skills of learning to tack in a dinghy. Computer simulations of great complexity will recreate the essential conditions of the oil rig emergency by showing screens representing and reacting like the actual control panels. The high-fidelity flight simulator creates a feeling that is indistinguishable from an actual flight. What the situations have in common is that it would be too complex, expensive, dangerous or just inconvenient to use the real thing for training.

Characteristics and associated training aids

The diversity of simulations makes it difficult to comment on the sort of training aids that would be appropriate, although as already mentioned, in some instances you may use a computer to present and control the simulation. In general terms, participants need to be clear about:

- which aspects of reality are being simulated
- what is expected of them
- which aspects of their performance need developing further.

To meet these needs, you might consider briefing sheets for use at the beginning of the simulation exercise, audio or video equipment to record what happens and self-assessment documentation at the end. As the simulation gets progressively more complex and technical, then your training aids will become more specialized.

Think carefully about the purpose of your simulation and therefore which aspects of reality need to be reproduced. Complete fidelity to the real situation is rarely necessary.

Case Studies

Case studies are widely used, particularly on management training courses, as material to provoke discussion and analysis, to explore attitudes, or to test understanding and the ability to tackle problems.

Characteristics
The material might be based on real or hypothetical events or situations and be presented as written material or on audio or video cassette. (As an example of the latter, BBC Enterprises have produced a series of three videos with the series title *Inside Organisations with Charles Handy*, featuring real companies and their staff, with commentary by Charles Handy.)

Although case-studies can be used by individuals learning on their own, trainers will find them most useful as a basis for group work. In this case, they could suffer from the same lack of focus as mentioned under 'Group Discussion' above.

Associated training aids
If you are using audio or video cassettes, then obviously you will need the equipment to play them on. In addition to this, you might also choose to video the group discussions.

In order to define the task, and introduce some structure into the discussion, you might consider producing a briefing sheet, containing key questions to be addressed and answered in relation to the case study material. Each group might find it useful to have their own flipchart, on which to summarize their discussions. This is useful both during the discussion, for the small group, and later too when they share their findings with their colleagues.

Guided Discovery Learning

Guided discovery learning is mainly used to learn concepts or principles (e.g. the relationship between electrical current and resistance in a circuit). The underlying principle is that given the right facilities and equipment, students can find things out for themselves, rather than being told by a trainer.

Characteristics

The instructor sets up a series of graded 'experiments' and gets learners to discover for themselves the underlying principles of what they observe and to draw conclusions from this. The trainer's role is to decide what tasks or 'experiments' to set, and at what stage to use them and then to construct them in detail. When the discovery process is under way, the trainer acts as a resource, answering questions posed by learners.

Associated training aids

As with simulation, the variety of situations in which guided discovery learning might be used makes it difficult to make general comments about appropriate training aids. Apart from anything needed for the 'experiments' (e.g. electrical circuit boards, equipment to be assembled, etc.), a well structured recording sheet would help learners to be systematic about recording the outcomes of what they do.

On-the-job Instruction

Many straightforward industrial or commercial tasks and procedures are taught 'on the job'. The office junior doesn't get sent on a training course in order to learn how to process an invoice – the procedure is explained in the office. Newcomers to the washing-machine assembly line are shown how to assemble the washing-machine within the production area of a factory. The apprentice learns how to change a wheel on a car when it next needs doing in the workshop. At managerial level, many aspects of a manager's work are taught through coaching on the job.

Characteristics

The learner is usually taught by a supervisor or a person skilled in the task being taught, but sometimes full-time or part-time instructors are used. Alternatively, the novice might be expected to pick things up from 'sitting-by-Nellie'. The major constraint is usually time. The supervisor or 'Nellie' have their own job to do, with the result that their instruction may be rushed or interrupted.

Associated training aids

The major purpose of training aids for on-the-job training is to compensate for the lack of time and attention that the instructor might give. As well as the normal tools and equipment used to do the job, the trainee would benefit from having other resources to refer to if necessary. If you want to improve on-the-job instruction, consider whether any of the following training aids would help:

- a simple checklist summarizing each stage of a procedure
- a diagrammatic illustration of a procedure, displayed near the equipment
- a tape-slide package, for studying when no one is available to consult
- a 'fault museum' to show quality standards and common faults.

Interactive Video (IV)

Interactive video combines computer controlled video sequences with computer-based instruction to produce highly effective training programmes in subjects ranging from statistical process control to assertiveness. To use the programmes, you need an interactive video workstation consisting of a micro computer with a special video display board, laser disc player and video monitor. Most companies use the IV stations solely for interactive video programmes, and a menu (list) of these will appear when the machine is switched on. However, it is possible to bypass this menu, and use the computer for general business applications such as word processing, spreadsheets and databases.

Characteristics

Interactive video is usually designed for individual study, though certain programmes have been created with group use in mind. In most cases, the programmes are largely self-contained, which means that all the information needed for the activities incorporated into the programme is available on the screen. Programmes differ in how easy it is to refer back to information presented in earlier sections.

Associated training aids

Because it has been a deliberate policy with certain producers to make their programmes self-contained, they have produced very little supporting documentation. This is a pity, because without reinforcement, the learning will atrophy. Things are changing though. Longman Training, for example, now produce a substantial self-study booklet to back up their IV programmes, and a detailed trainer's guide to a follow-up course in which learners can put into practice the skills covered in the IV. If you choose to incorporate IV into your training programmes, you might consider producing your own summary notes or find other ways of reinforcing the contents.

An alternative way of looking at IV material is to regard it as a training aid, rather than a self-contained training package. The programmes dealing with behavioural skills, for example, are a rich source of vignettes which provide excellent illustrations of different aspects of behaviour. You can access them easily if you get to grips with software such as PC Opensoft. This is described in detail in Chapter 7.

TRAINER'S TIP

Be imaginative in your use of training aids. Material designed for one purpose may be usefully adapted for another.

Computer-Based Training (CBT)

As with IV, most computer-based training is designed for self-study. It is used for a range of training applications including tutorials, drill and practice (e.g. keyboard skills), simulations (e.g. fault-finding on a central heating system), and covers both technical and behavioural subjects. Applications have been developed for classroom use, but these are in highly technical and complex subjects.

As far as the more modest applications are concerned, CBT's potential as a training aid is underexploited. Many of the programs will contain exercises that could well be done in the classroom. Where calculations are based on putting figures into a standard formula, there may be scope for demonstrating the effects of different projections (e.g. the effect of different rates of inflation on the value of a pension).

Characteristics
The speed and accuracy with which the computer responds makes it a valuable resource in the training room.

Associated training aids
If you want your group to be able to see what is on the computer monitor, you have three options:

- to link your monitor with others in the training room so that each trainee has a clear view of a screen

      – to replace the normal monitor with a larger version
      – to use a computer projection system.

Apart from the hardware, consider what sort of documentation, if any, would be 'useful to the learners'.

Project Work

Project work is an important part of many training programmes leading to a qualification, particularly for managers and supervisors. The project is seen as a way of putting into practice some of the more theoretical parts of the training course.

Characteristics

Learners complete the project on their own, and then submit it for comment, sometimes to a manager in their own department.

Associated training aids

Here is an instance where the phrase 'training aids' could well be replaced by 'learning aids'. The value of the project lies not just in doing it and writing it up, but also in the feedback that it generates when it's complete. Whoever reviews the project has an opportunity for helping the trainee to learn from what they've done. Giving constructive feedback is an art in which levels of skills differ. To help maximize the learning that accrues from a project, you might consider providing guidelines on feedback for those who give it. You would be helping them to help the learner learn.

Group Exercises

Group exercises include such things as Fishbowl, Lego building, team-building activities, etc. Group activities such as these don't fall neatly into the category of group discussion, nor of simulation. Their purpose is to provide a context in which to experiment with various issues to do with group work.

Characteristics

Any group activity puts pressure on the trainer to be absolutely clear about the aims of the activity and the conditions under which the activity will run. This is particularly important when several groups will all be doing a similar activity at the same time. If members of a group feel that they understood the brief differently from another group, or if they were unclear about the purpose, then resentment against the trainer can build up and the potential for learning from the experience evaporates.

Associated training aids

To help people learn from their experience of doing the activity, check that your supporting documentation is easy to read and totally unambiguous. Provide guidance on what to look for, if you are using observers, and encourage each participant to complete a self-assessment sheet. These can be used as the basis for discussion of the activity.

Training method	Training aid							
	White board	OHP	Audio tape	Video/ film	Job aid	Hand-out	Simulator	Computer/ IV equip
Presentation	✓	✓	✓	✓		✓		✓
Group discussion	✓					✓		
Demonstration		✓		✓	✓		✓	
Role play				✓		✓		
Simulation				✓			✓	✓
Case study	✓	✓		✓		✓		
Discovery learning					✓	✓	✓	
On-the-job instruction					✓			
IV/CBT						✓		✓
Project work		✓					✓	
Group process activities	✓			✓		✓		

Figure 3.1 *Training aids most commonly used with different training methods*

Part 2 Using Training Aids

4 Whiteboards and Flipcharts

<table>
<tr><td>▷</td><td align="center">SUMMARY</td><td>◁</td></tr>
</table>

This chapter:
- Describes the use of whiteboards and flipcharts.
- Explains the techniques for using them effectively.

Whiteboards

A whiteboard is a board with a white surface for writing on. Is there anything more to say? Certainly, the whiteboard is such a simple, familiar and ubiquitous piece of equipment that it would seem to need little introduction. However, it's given a section of its own here because there are some differences between the different boards available, and because whiteboards (or chalkboards, or green boards) are often not used to their best advantage.

Description of the Equipment

Whiteboards vary in size between the personal notepad version to the huge wall-mounted expanses that you will find in certain tailor-made training suites. However, the most significant differences between one whiteboard and another aren't apparent until you start to use them. Most boards currently in use have a 'dry-wipe' surface: this means that they will wipe clean with any soft cloth or felt board rubber – provided of course, that you have used the correct dry-marker pens. You may still come across boards that have to be cleaned with water, or with special board cleaner.

Certain whiteboards have a vitreous enamel surface on a steel backing and therefore are magnetic. On these boards you can use magnets to display sheets from the flipchart, which is useful when there are no display rails in the room and you cannot fix things on to the walls. Another possible application is to use the board as a surface on which to attach magnets representing objects to be moved into different positions.

You will also come across whiteboards that have a photocopying facility. Just press a button, and whatever is marked on the board at the time will be reproduced on A4-sized paper.

Training Applications

Most wall-mounted, or free-standing whiteboards are a generous size, and offer you plenty of space for making spontaneous notes to complement what you are saying, or to summarize the contributions from your course members. Work carefully when you use it, though; you could find yourself running out of space before you are ready to delete what is already written. It might seem that the photocopying whiteboards would come into their own here, but in fact their usefulness would be limited. It's usually the participants who would need a record of the contents of the board, and it's unlikely that you would want to hold things up to take a copy for each of them.

Preparation

The beauty of the whiteboard is that it's there, ready for use. All you have to do is to check that you have a supply of dry-marker pens, and something with which to clean the board.

Good Training Practice

Layout
Because you have so much space, and will tend to use the whiteboard without preparation, you are likely to end up with a jumbled display of unconnected words or diagrams. The following guidelines will help you avoid this.

- Mentally divide the board into two or three vertical segments, and use one segment at a time. Sentences that straggle across the whole width of the board will be difficult to read, and invariably will be crooked.

- Erase information that is no longer relevant.
- Put up headings, to focus attention on what is being recorded.
- Use different colours to identify related information.

Legibility

Use a marker that gives a line thick enough to be seen easily by the person sitting furthest away from the board. Check this in advance. Practise writing with the marker, too, because the slipperiness of the board makes writing difficult to control.

Talking and writing

Talk to your audience, not to the board. Discipline yourself to stop talking while you are writing things up. When you start talking again, stand to one side of the board so that you don't get in the way of what you have written.

Flipcharts

The informality and flexibility of the flipchart have made it one of the most widely available visual aids, both inside and outside the training room. It is extremely simple to use once you know the various tricks of the trade that make it effective.

Description of the Equipment

The flipchart is simply a portable tripod or easel supporting an A1-sized pad of paper. The legs of the tripod will retract, so that the frame can stand on a desk. Without the paper, most current models can be used as a whiteboard. As an alternative to pads of paper, you may prefer the reusable plastic coated sheets. These wipe clean and are durable enough to be used over and over again.

Training Applications

The flipchart is essentially an informal training aid, and is most effective when used with small groups. Use it to display prepared material, or else to record, illustrate, or reinforce what you or your course members say. Individual sheets can be detached and displayed on the walls and referred to throughout the course, which is particularly helpful for things like participants' objectives.

Preparation

Like the whiteboard, the flipchart itself needs the minimum of setting up. Check that you have an adequate supply of paper and different coloured pens, together with any prepared material and you're ready to go.

Production of Materials

If you know that you will need to display information such as the key points of a particular session, summaries, instructions for activities etc., then it's worth writing these up in advance. You'll produce a neater result and it will save time during the course.

You will get a well balanced effect if you draft the layout on a piece of A4 paper, and then scale it up for A1. Either use flipchart paper that has a grid lightly printed on it, or else draw some guidelines yourself and erase them when you've finished. If your company has invested in the technology, you can create an A4 master – either manually or printed out from a computer – and use a poster printer to create an A1-sized version of it to display on your flipchart.

Good Training Practice

Legibility

As with any display medium, your first concern is that people can read what you have written. Writing that is legible to you standing in front of the flipchart may be impossibly small for people sitting further away. You might also find that your writing gets smaller and the line droops as you approach the edge of the paper. Check before your audience arrives that what you write can be read comfortably from the back of the room and that your lines of writing are reasonably straight.

Layout

If you are using the flipchart to display key points, or a summary of what you have discussed, then three or four well spaced items will be sufficient. Anything more begins to lose its impact.

If you are recording the outcome of, say, a discussion or a brainstorming session, then you can afford to put more on each sheet. Avoid the very bottom of the sheet, though. It may be difficult to see from the back of the room.

Identification

A heading at the top of every sheet will help your group to focus on the current topic. It will also help you to pick out the relevant pages if you need to refer back to something.

If you spread onto two or more sheets, then put a '. . . contd' heading and a page number. It's obvious at the time what the contents refer to, but can be puzzling later when you're looking for something specific.

When you know that you will come back to a particular sheet at some later stage, stick a tag on it, or turn up the corner, so that it's easily identifiable.

Use of colour

Using a range of strong colours will enhance the effect of your display. If you are working on prepared sheets, then you will be able to use different colours consistently for different purposes – for example: headings, key words, explanations. Avoid pale colours like yellow, because they don't show up well.

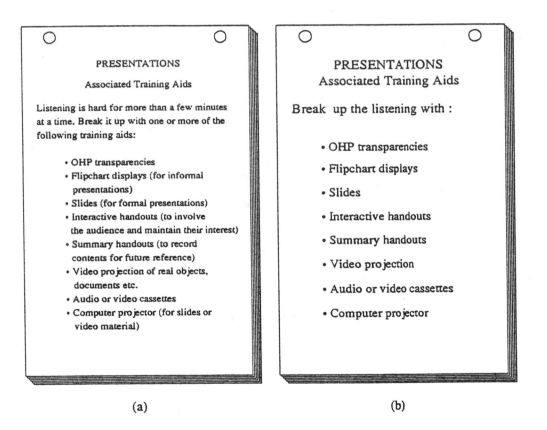

(a)   (b)

Figure 4.1 *Two versions of the same material written on a flipchart*

Contents

The flipchart is the place for short, sharp messages. Write only the key words; leave out all the inessential words, and use abbreviations. Keep your complete sentences and explanations for your handouts. Using the flipchart, you have got neither the time nor the space to be discursive. The two versions in Figure 4.1 illustrate this.

Talking and writing

As with the whiteboard, you have to turn away from your audience in order to write on the flipchart. Don't keep on talking. The silence may seem long to you, but participants will be reading and thinking about what you're putting up. To them, the few seconds silence will be a welcome respite. When you do start talking again, stand to one side of the flipchart, not in front of it.

Relevance

Any visual medium that you use should display only images that are relevant to what you are talking about at the time. With an overhead projector it's good practice to switch the machine off once you've finished referring to a transparency. With a slide projector, you show a 'fill-in' slide that provides something restful to look at without conveying any new information. With the flipchart, you simply turn to a blank page.

If you are using a sequence of prepared pages, then leave a blank sheet between them. This provides the break between the page you have finished with, and the next one that you are not quite ready for.

The very familiarity of the flipchart means it's often used as a scribble pad. It will be more effective if you use it with a particular purpose in mind.

5 Projectors

▷   SUMMARY   ◁

This chapter:
- Describes the key features of a range of overhead projection equipment.
- Explains how to design and produce attention-getting transparencies.

The Overhead Projector (OHP)

Next to the flipchart and the whiteboard, the overhead projector (OHP) is one of the most commonly used training aids. It has two main advantages over other means for displaying visual material: firstly it can be used in normal daylight conditions without the need for blackout, and secondly the tutor can use it and continue to face the audience. OHP transparencies can be prepared in advance, or the tutor can use a roll of acetate or acetate sheets, together with special fibre-tip OHP pens, during a training session.

Description of the Equipment

The OHP

The projector consists of a light source and a mirror/lens system that projects an image of a transparency onto any form of white screen. The projection area and hence the transparency is usually 10" × 10" (255 mm × 255 mm) or, with more modern projectors, A4 square (285 mm × 285 mm).

Figure 5.1 shows a range of typical OHPs. Figure 5.1(a) is the standard projector that can be found in most training rooms. It has a large body containing the light source, a mirror and a Fresnel lens (a large glass screen on which you place the transparency). The projection head containing a lens and mirror arrangement is mounted on a fixed support. The projection head can normally be moved up or down the head support to focus the image, and the mirror can usually be rotated to adjust the height of the projected image.

A more portable version with a retractable head support and carrying handle is shown in Figure 5.1(b). This works in a similar way to the standard OHP, with the light source, mirror and Fresnel lens contained in the large base, and a lens and mirror system mounted in the head. These models are useful where you need to retract the head when the projector isn't in use (for example, when you want to show a 35 mm slide) or you regularly need to move the OHP to a different room.

Figure 5.1(c) shows a Fresnel mirror system that is more portable still. In this model, the light source is mounted inside the projector head. The base contains a Fresnel mirror that reflects the image back into the head. The image is in turn projected through the head and on to the screen. The head and head support retracts, and the whole projector can often be packed into a small carrying case, making it ideal for moving between different locations.

If you are buying an overhead projector, your main considerations must be whether it will project the right sized image for the space you have available, and whether the quality of the image is suitable for your purpose. You may have a fixed position for the OHP and the screen, with limited space in between, in which case you will need a wide angle lens (e.g. 270 mm) to get a full sized image on the screen.

Once these basic considerations are taken care of, then you can consider the importance of having features such as:

- a scratch-resistant coating on the Fresnel lens
- a collapsible column
- two lamps, so that if one fails, you can instantly switch to the spare
- register pins, to keep transparencies in place on the platen
- the option of using a continuous roll of transparency, rather than individual sheets
- an electrical output socket for connecting with other equipment
- a silent, or almost silent, heat dissipation system

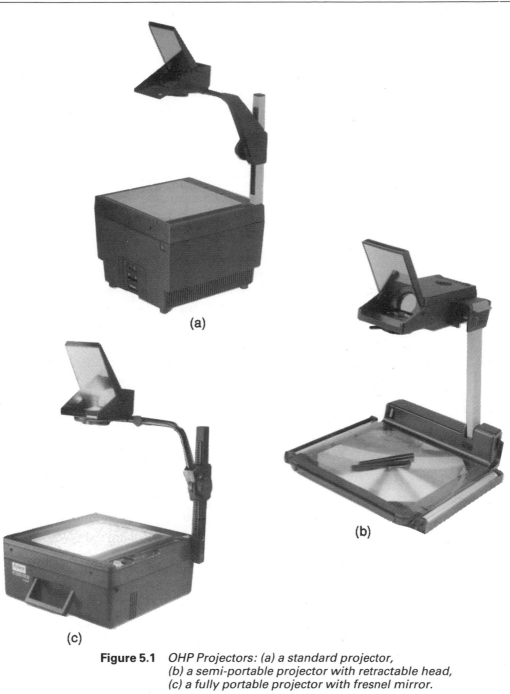

(a)

(b)

(c)

Figure 5.1 *OHP Projectors: (a) a standard projector,
(b) a semi-portable projector with retractable head,
(c) a fully portable projector with fresnel mirror.*

49

- light weight (5-7 kg for the most portable, as opposed to 9-11 kg for the conventional tabletop models)
- the facility to zoom in on any part of your document
- a 'condenser lens' to boost light output, and give extra definition when using the OHP in bright daylight, or with multiple overlays.

Screens

Portable or fixed?

To many trainers, the OHP screen is a cumbersome three legged beast that lurks in the corner of almost every training room, defying attempts to move it without causing havoc.

This type of screen is certainly the most common because it has the advantage of folding up into a neat, portable package (though unpacking them can be a severe test for the uninitiated). If you work in a room used solely for training, you may have the alternative – screens suspended from the ceiling or mounted on the wall, operated mechanically, electrically or by remote radio control. You may even have the model that extends sideways instead of up or down.

The 'keystone effect'

Regardless of how the screen is mounted, it will have a means of tilting it away from the vertical, to avoid the *keystone effect*. This is the distorted, wedge-shaped image illustrated in Figure 5.2(a). It arises because the screen has to be higher than the projector in order for the image to be visible. The projector head therefore has to be angled upwards in order to throw the image on to the screen, with the result that the top part of the image is further away from the projector than the bottom. To compensate for this, the screen is tilted so that it's at right angles to the projector. This equalizes the distances (see Figure 5.2(b)) and balances the image. The means of achieving this is simple. Most screens hang from a notched bracket. Changing the position on the bracket will alter the angle of the screen. Some wall or ceiling mounted screens are fixed at the top, but vary the angle of the screen by pulling it away from the vertical from the bottom. The effect is the same.

Quality of the image

The quality of the projected image is determined not only by the projector and ambient light conditions, but also by the surface of the screen. Sales information tends to give highly technical data about the benefits of different coatings, but basically what the manufacturers are trying to do is to increase the brightness of the image (they call it the *photometric efficiency*). When buying a new screen, try out

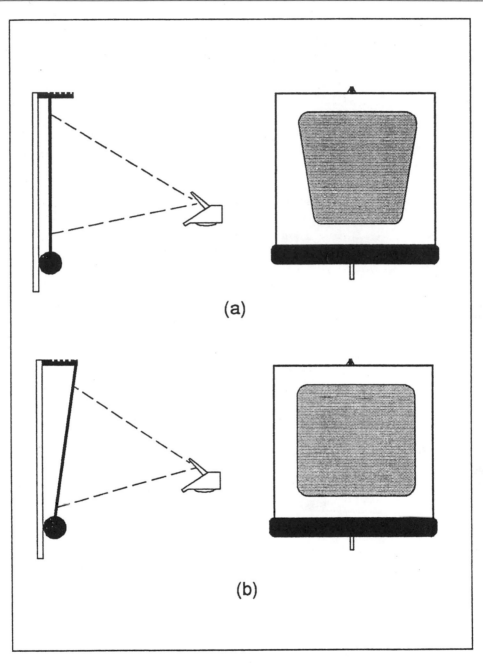

Figure 5.2 *(a) Keystone effect on OHP projection*
(b) eliminated by tilting the screen

the different types using your own equipment and in your own working environment, to see which best suits your particular conditions.

OHP transparencies

One blank OHP transparency looks very much like another, but in fact those that you can write on yourself are not the same as those suitable for use in printers or photocopiers. Broadly speaking, the latter are:

- treated with antistatic, to ease their progress through the paper feed
- heat resistant, so that they emerge flat
- specially coated, to make the ink or toner adhere better to their surface

Manufacturers produce a range of transparencies (both clear and coloured), and specify the machines on which each product should be used.

To help you add colour to your presentations, manufacturers also supply 'colour edge' photocopier film. This is produced in a range of tints and has a more densely coloured border around the edge of the sheet.

OHP pens

With OHP pens, your first choice is between permanent or non-permanent markers. After that, artistic and practical considerations will determine the width of the tip and the colours you use.

Permanent inks dry quickly and are waterproof and smudge-resistant. They can be removed from almost all smooth surfaces with an alcohol-based solvent. For cleaning large areas, use the solvent on a cloth or tissue. For greater precision, use a solvent correction pen, or a special eraser. With either, the erased surface can be remarked immediately.

Non-permanent inks take slightly longer to dry completely. Once dry, they too resist smudging but not to the same extent as permanent inks. Handle with care, because perspiration from your fingers can make them look messy. The ink is easily removed with water, but again, for more accurate erasing, use a special eraser.

Both permanent and non-permanent inks will keep their colours on the transparencies in normal use, but will gradually fade if they are exposed to sun or ultraviolet light over long periods.

Liquid crystal data panels

If you are adept at using graphics software, but frustrated by the limitations of the printout as a means of producing transparencies, then there is a technological alternative (at a price). The liquid crystal data panel is a device that sits on the platen of the OHP. It is connected to a computer by a cable and it reproduces the contents of the computer screen. The light from the OHP shines through the palette and projects the image on to the OHP screen. Depending on the model you chose, this image can be in shades of grey or in colour.

Training Applications

OHP or flipchart?

The overhead projector is sometimes used as an alternative to the flipchart, but although their uses do overlap, one is by no means a substitute for the other.

Transparencies have the edge over the flipchart when you can afford the time to produce something visually impressive. Because you can photocopy or print on to transparencies, you can tap into the enormous range of ready made or computer generated material. The variety of fonts on some word processors and printers will transform the most ordinary list of bullet points into an interesting and memorable image.

Achieving the same effects on a flipchart would require the skills of a sign writer or an artist – or rather it did until recently. Technology now gives you another option: if you invest in a poster printer, you can take an A4 original and reproduce it on A1 paper in two colours (single colour print on a different coloured background). This certainly can achieve striking effects, but it is expensive and you might still prefer OHP transparencies simply because they are easier to store and re-use.

When you need to record things quickly, or produce a spontaneous illustration, then the flipchart comes into its own. It's less slippery to write on and there's more space. You can also display the relevant sheets around the room for reference.

Prepared OHP transparencies

Every training course has a mixture of prepared and spontaneous elements. For those parts that are predictable, prepare transparencies to:

- signpost the main topics in a presentation
- summarize key points in a section
- summarize the main features of the presentation
- present important facts and figures that feature in your talk
- add humour (by showing a cartoon)
- emphasize points with suitable illustrations and embellishments.

53

Spontaneous use of transparencies

Create new transparencies spontaneously when you:

— think a diagram would clarify something you are saying
— want to note the points that the group are making
— need to note some key points of your own if you are moving into areas for which you haven't already prepared transparencies.

Preparation

The projector

How it works

Before you start using the projector, check that you are familiar with the basic principles of how it works. This means knowing how to:

— make the projected image larger or smaller (move the projector away from or closer to the screen).
— raise or lower the image on the screen (alter the angle of the head).
— eliminate the wedge shaped distortion of the image, both vertically and horizontally (tilt the screen to eliminate the keystone effect, i.e. the vertical distortion; set the projector at right angles to the screen to eliminate the horizontal distortion).
— focus the image (move the head up or down the column).
— change a lamp if it blows (switch over to the standby if the projector has one, or else change the bulb – make sure you always carry a spare). Be careful not to knock the machine when it's on as this could make the lamp blow.

Positioning the OHP

In some training rooms, the screen and projector are permanently fixed. Assuming that the distance between the two projects an image large enough to be seen at the back of the seating area, the fixed position makes things easier for you. All you have to do is find the on/off switch, and check the focus.

Problems can arise, though, if the projector is at one or other end of your desk or table. A fixture on your far left is awkward to write on if you are right-handed; a fixture on the right is similarly awkwardly placed for left-handers. If you have had to move to an extreme position, some of your audience may have to turn their chairs to see you.

If the position of the OHP and screen is flexible, then obviously you will set it in a position that is convenient for you, but an equally important consideration is the comfort of your audience. Their basic requirement is an unimpeded view of what you intend them to see. The most likely obstacles are you and the OHP column, so project the image high on the screen and keep out of the way.

Once these basics are taken care of, consider the size of the projection. To produce an image of 1 metre (39 inches) square, the distance between the projector and the screen would need to be between 1.3 m (52 inches) and 1.8 m (69 inches) depending on the type of OHP in use. Moving the projector away from the screen increases the size of the image by roughly the same amount. Figure 5.3(c) shows these sizes for a typical projector with a standard lens.

	Size of lens(mm)		
	270	317	355
1.0	1.32	1.57	1.76
1.5	1.84	2.19	2.46
3..0	3.42	4.07	4.56

Image size (M)

Distance from screen
for different lenses

(a)

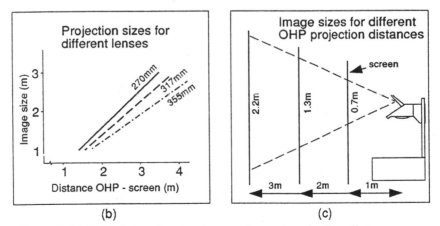

(b)   (c)

Figure 5.3   *OHP slides showing image size and projection distance*
(a) as a table, (b) as a graph for different lenses
and (c) as a diagram for a standard 317mm lens

55

Designing transparencies

Purpose

The purpose of transparencies is to emphasize and reinforce what you say and to add interest and variety. But they are transitory – displayed briefly and then removed – so go for immediate impact. It's this more than anything that will determine their success.

Making transparencies easy to read

The fundamental rule is to keep them simple. The information on each should complement what you say, be easily understood and confined to what is strictly relevant at the time. If you need a degree of complexity, then build it up stage by stage, rather than displaying it all at once.

Bear the following in mind when writing your transparencies to ensure that they are easy to read:

- use a mixture of upper and lower case letters: upper case alone takes longer to read
- separate one point from another by leaving plenty of space in between
- position your words/diagrams so that they are framed by white space, i.e. the transparency is not too cluttered
- limit the amount of information: if you are using words, then a maximum of ten lines and six or seven words per line is a useful rule of thumb to avoid overcrowding the image
- use letters that can be seen even by short-sighted people sitting at the back of the group (probably a minimum of 6 mm ($\frac{1}{4}$ inch) high, and solidly formed, but check for yourself beforehand what is big enough for your training room)
- try using reversed out images, either white or colours on a black background as in Fig 5.4(b) to add emphasis.

Making transparencies memorable

You will help people remember the information you are trying to impart if you bear the following in mind when preparing your transparencies:

- start with a heading, so that people have got a concept to relate to
- use colour to highlight important words, to add variety and interest and to increase the visual impact (but avoid yellow, because it's difficult to see)
- liven up your display with a selective use of speech bubbles, jagged lines around words, exclamation marks, etc. (see Figure 5.5)

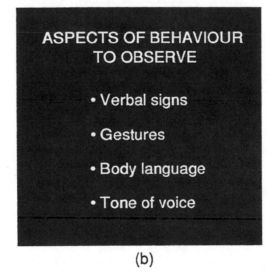

(b)

Figure 5.4 *Background colour on OHP transparencies*

    – use key words to reinforce what you are saying
    – use graphical ways of putting across information
    – keep your message brief.

Check that your transparencies fit the exposure area; you don't want to have to move the slide up and down.

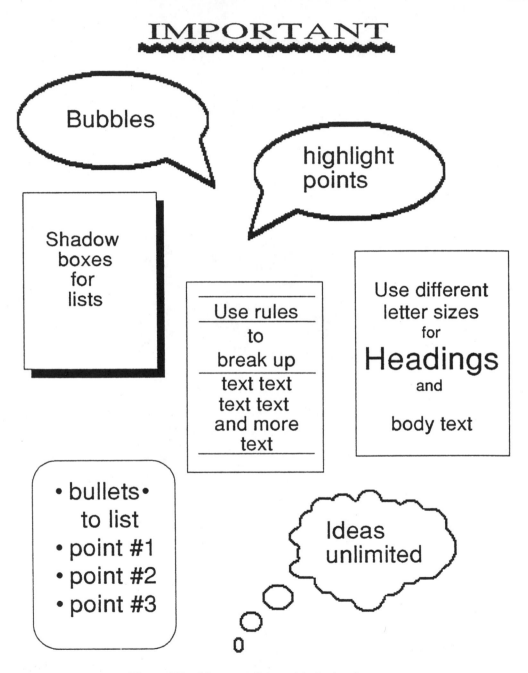

Figure 5.5 *Liven up slides with design features*

Words or pictures?

The beauty of transparencies is that they add a visual dimension to what you are saying. But if you include only words, however beautifully laid out and coloured, you are not exploiting the potential of the OHP. Try adding something more graphic, especially for prepared transparencies. You'll find a wealth of ready drawn images and illustrations all ready for printing out if you investigate the range of 'clip art' available for computer use. Clip art is free from copyright restrictions. Much of it will be public domain, and so very modestly priced, though you'll also come across disks at commercial rates. Some examples of clip art you might find useful are shown in Figure 5.6.

Figure 5.6 *Use clip art with desktop publishing software to produce imaginative slides and transparencies*

If your courses are run very informally, and you don't feel under pressure to produce professional looking transparencies, then try a few sketches yourself. You don't need to be an artist. The most primitive drawings can be surprisingly effective. If they make your audience laugh, so much the better. You'll have made your point. Not all visuals are free hand drawings, though. Diagrams, bar charts and graphs are perhaps easier to produce, and equally effective, especially if they encapsulate information that otherwise would be hard to digest. Take as an example the table in Figure 5.3(a). It contains two main messages: that the size of a projected image is determined by the size of lens in the projector and also by the distance between the projector and the screen. These messages are more clearly conveyed in graphical form as in Figure 5.3(b). But even this contains a lot of information. Simplify things further by taking just one lens and portraying the information as in Figure 5.3(c). This version of the information is much easier to understand and remember. It clarifies rather than overwhelms. A separate slide can be used to show the effect of using different sized lenses.

Techniques of production
Production techniques for OHP transparencies range from spontaneous pen-on-acetate scribbles to expensive, studio-produced, full-colour works of art. Your choice will depend on:

- the time available
- the expectations of your audience
- the number of times you will use the same transparencies
- your budget
- the equipment available to you, and your ability to use it, or the availability of personnel who can
- your awareness of the options.

Some of the possibilities have already been referred to in this chapter. For easy reference, the main alternatives have been drawn together and described below.
By hand Writing directly on to a piece of acetate is certainly the easiest and quickest way of producing your transparencies in advance. Using rub-on lettering is much more time consuming but will produce a neater effect. If you bear in mind the design guidelines, the results of either method can be good enough for use in informal situations. To get the best results, make a few preliminary sketches to decide on the best layout. Without this preparation, the result will probably be a mess.

It will help if you lay your sheet of acetate on to a grid so that your writing is straight and evenly spaced. You can also use the grid to define your borders, so that your artwork is framed by white space.

Photocopying Using the photocopier extends your options. It means you can put together a mixture of self-generated, computer-generated and other ready-made material on a sheet of paper, and photocopy the result on to an acetate.

Thermal copying Depending on the film used, thermal copiers can produce black images on a clear or tinted background, coloured images on a clear background or a clear white image on an opaque background.

Lettering machines You could get more professional looking artwork by replacing your handwriting with strips of self-adhesive letters produced on a lettering machine. Stick the self-adhesive strips into position on paper, supplement it with other artwork and photocopy the result on the acetate.

A more complex version of these lettering machines, with a typewriter-style keyboard, can print text or graphics horizontally or vertically on to A4 paper or transparency. It offers nine different character sizes (up to 36 point in Helvetica Bold) and three type styles in four different colours. Other models, more sophisticated still, are available for those whose need for professional looking output can justify the investment.

Computer printed transparencies The versatility of desk-top publishing and graphics software, and even of certain word processing packages, offers enormous scope for producing striking layouts from a computer. If you haven't got access to a colour printer, you can transform the black and white output by hand colouring with different coloured OHP pens.

Design studio production If you are delivering training or presentations to audiences who have grown accustomed to professional quality visual aids, your credibility may suffer if you offer them anything less. In this case, it may be worth commissioning a design studio, or your own design department if you have one, to produce your transparencies for you. The cost of this becomes more worthwhile if you are going to be using the same transparencies many times.

Good Training Practice

The equipment holds no surprises for you and you have a pile of attention-grabbing transparencies in front of you. Your task now is to incorporate them seamlessly into your training. The message they project is the important thing; the mechanics of projecting it should be unnoticable.

Here you come up against Murphy's Law: if something can go wrong, it will! This has special significance for trainers using visual aids because there are so many pitfalls. Fortunately for your peace of mind, there are some simple precautions you can take to avoid chaos, and these are explained below.

Framing

Single sheets of acetate are slippery and difficult to handle. No matter how carefully you interleave them with paper, it's difficult to sort through them and pick out the one you want. The solution is to mount each transparency in a frame. You have the choice between a robust card frame or a transparent plastic envelope such as the Flipframe™. Both are universally punched so that they fit on to the retaining pins on the OHP itself. Card frames keep the transparency tight and flat, but their additional bulk means that you need a frame box or large ring binder to store them in. Flipframes™ fit into an ordinary ring binder.

References

Framing your transparencies not only makes them easier to store, it also means that there is somewhere to note a reference number, an identification mark or a brief reminder to yourself. If Murphy strikes, and your pile of transparencies is knocked on to the floor just before a session, you won't panic if they have been numbered beforehand – you can put them back in order without any difficulty.

Where to put them

Once you have identified each transparency with a number, you need to keep them in order while you are using them. Ideally, you should give yourself space to keep unused transparencies on one side of the projector, and the ones you have displayed on the other side, still in order. If you need to refer again to something you have already shown, you will be able to find it quickly.

Displaying the transparencies

Trainers sometimes fail to do justice to their transparencies simply because they are sloppy in the way they display them. The following procedure will keep your audience's attention focused on the screen, rather than distracting them with the mechanics of using the OHP.

1. Before switching on the OHP, lay the transparency on the platen. Check that it's straight and the right way up. If you have made a mistake, only you will have seen it.
2. Switch on the OHP.

3. Talk through the contents or allow time for the audience to read the contents of the transparency and make notes as appropriate.
4. Switch off the OHP. Your audience doesn't want to look at a transparency that's no longer relevant to what's being said.
5. Remove the transparency and put it face down on the pile of those already displayed.

Keeping eye contact

One of the major advantages of the OHP is that you don't need to turn away from your audience in order to use it. So long as you have checked the position of the projector in relation to the screen before you start, you can be confident that a transparency that is correctly aligned on the platen will throw a well-placed image on to the screen.

If you need to refer to the contents of the transparency while you're talking, then read off the OHP. Don't turn away from your audience and talk at the screen. Similarly, when you want to draw attention to a particular part of your transparency, point directly at it on the platen (with a slim marker) instead of pointing towards the screen.

Using a pointer

Your audience will need time to register which part of the transparency you are referring to, so a vague gesture of the hand, throwing an ambiguous shadow on the screen won't be sufficient. Something more specific is needed.

You *can* use your finger to point with, but you'll have to stand close to the projector to point accurately, which means you'll probably prevent people seeing the screen. The most readily available alternative is a well-sharpened, straight-sided pencil. (A round one will roll out of position.) Lay it on the platen, pointing precisely at the appropriate part of the transparency, and then step back out of the way.

Alternatively, you could use a telescopic pointer. This has the advantage of allowing you to point to several different things in succession, without having to move close to the projector.

What do you say?

No one can listen and read at the same time. If you put up a transparency and immediately start talking, your audience will either ignore you and read the transparency, ignore the transparency and listen to you, or let their attention jump backwards and forwards. None of these is as efficient as allowing them to concentrate on doing one thing at a time.

When you switch on the OHP, pause for a few seconds. You can judge the length of your silence by reading (inwardly) what you've displayed as though you are seeing it for the first time. Then wait just a little longer before you say anything.

When you do speak, don't just repeat what is already on the OHP. This tends to happen if the transparency is being used as a prompt. But because the contents of the transparency will be a highly compressed version of normal speech, it sounds strange if you read them aloud. Quite apart from that, your audience will have read things for themselves, and your repetition will add nothing.

Display techniques

The OHP has an advantage over the slide projector in that you can decide how you reveal the contents. You can keep your audience's attention focused on particular points by concealing the rest with a piece of paper.

If you slide the paper under the transparency, it will mean that you can still see the later points, but they will not be displayed on the screen until you move the paper. Alternatively, use semi-transparent paper on top, which you can see through, but which casts a shadow on the screen.

If you have a linear list of points, you can reveal them one by one by sliding the paper down. If you have parts of a diagram to conceal, then cover them with a flap of paper attached to the transparency (see Figure 5.7).

Alternatively, you may need to start with a basic diagram and progressively add information. You can do this with overlays. Figure 5.8 provides a very simple example. More complex graphs, tables or diagrams can be built up in a similar way.

Yet another option is to prepare a master transparency using permanent ink, and to add to it as you talk, with water-soluble ink. Wipe away your additions after your session, and the original is ready to be used again.

Episcopes and Video OHPs

Description of the Equipment

If you want to display original documents, then you could photograph them. Alternatively, you might turn to an episcope – a modern version of the old epidiascope.

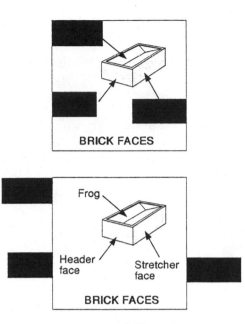

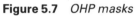

Figure 5.7 *OHP masks*

Figure 5.8 *OHP overlays*

Episcopes

The early models of the episcope used to be large and cumbersome pieces of equipment that needed powerful and therefore noisy fans and blackout conditions in which to operate. Their justification is that they can project any form of visual material, and even small objects, that will fit on the platen. Since the space above the platen is very limited, the size of the objects is severely restricted.

Modern versions have the same function, and are justified on the grounds that they save you time in producing slides or OHP transparencies – you just use the original instead. (This of course presumes that you have an original that you don't first have to produce.) Modern technology has meant that the disadvantage of size has now been overcome; current models weigh around 12 kg and are truly portable. However, they still need the room to be blacked out.

Video OHPS

The electronic version of the episcope – the video OHP – has the advantage of operating in normal light conditions, and of allowing you to display objects of much greater depth. But convenience has its price. You will need a generous budget and/or a very pressing need for what the technology allows you to do.

In the video OHP (see Figure 5.9), the source of light of the traditional OHP is replaced by a high resolution camera head pointing down at an object on the platen. The object can be anything you like – a book or some form of documentation, a circuit board, a model of a building. Whatever the camera focuses on – static or moving – will be displayed.

A variation on the same theme is the Wolf Visualizer. Instead of the camera head looking down on the object, there is a reflector head doing the same thing, and the camera is in the base. A zoom facility allows you to display any part of the object.

TRAINER'S TIP

Technology can be seductive and impressive, but will it help people to learn? Make sure you have a good reason for using a training aid and allow plenty of time for setting it up.

Training Applications

The technical niceties are less important here than what the machine will do for you. The machine will be useful to you if you regularly need to:

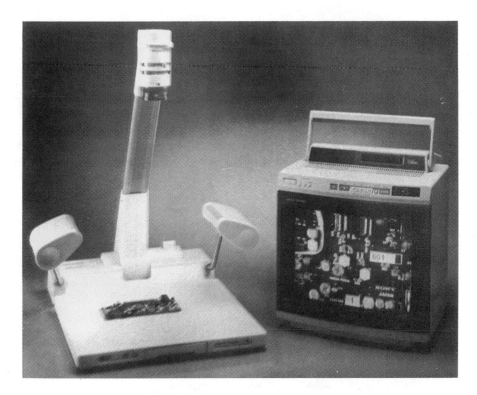

Figure 5.9 *A video OHP. A video camera is mounted in the head, illumination is provided by a light on either side of the platen, and the image is viewed on a monitor or a video projector.*

- project three-dimensional objects, particularly when it isn't feasible to provide individual objects for each course member to look at
- project in full colour from an original document, rather than from a photocopy
- link up with video monitors or a computer
- transmit to different locations via a satellite.

Preparation

As with an ordinary OHP, your priority is to check that you know how the equipment works.

Production of Materials

The beauty of this equipment is that you don't need to prepare special materials. You are working with the originals.

67

Good Training Practice

The more complex the object you are displaying, the more important it is to be very definite about what you are pointing to, and to hold the pointer in place long enough for your audience to take in the details.

The standard rules of switching on and off apply here, as does the need to keep out of the way of the projection. You will also need to explain carefully what you are displaying and why.

Equip yourself with a telescopic pointer because if you want to examine items in detail, you will need to identify specific features of them. An alternative is a hand-held laser pointer, which will project a laser beam onto the screen and highlight a feature with a red dot. As well as their precision, another of their advantages is that you can use them from different parts of the room, as you move around. You don't have to return to the source of light in order to throw a shadow on to the screen. It might be worth considering a laser pointer if you think you'd have sufficient use to justify the cost.

Slide Projectors

For most training purposes, OHP transparencies are a flexible and convenient form of visual aid. But if your audience is accustomed to, and expects, the highest quality projected images, anything less than slides could be regarded as unprofessional.

This section covers the use of slide projection to support a presentation. The use of tape/slide programmes involves more complex equipment and is dealt with in the next chapter.

Description of the Equipment

Slide Projectors

As with almost every training aid mentioned in this book, the range of equipment is enormous. However, the basic principle is the same. A selected slide is slotted in front of a light and an image is projected through a lens on to a screen.

Assuming that your training courses don't need synchronized multiple projectors and electronic dissolves, the features likely to be most significant to you are:

- the size of the lens
- a remote control facility
- sufficient power to project well in less than total blackout.

The first of these – the size of lens – becomes important when the projector has to be mounted within a few feet of the screen. You will need a wide angled lens in order to get an image of an acceptable size. The second – the remote control facility – means that you don't have to worry about getting in the way of the projected image when you change a slide. It is also useful for trainers who don't like to be tied to standing in one place. Finally, if you can project strong images without needing to black out the room, then it's more convenient for both you and your audience.

The slides themselves may be produced photographically or by computer. The production process is discussed briefly later in this chapter.

Projection of computer images

If you are using computer software to design slides, then you could bypass the process of turning your computer output into a slide by projecting an image directly from the computer itself. There are numerous computer presentation software packages on the market that are designed to control the sequence and timing of your presentation, and a look at suppliers' catalogues will give you a good idea of what's available.

Having designed your slides on the computer, you then have to decide how to display them. If your audience is small, the computer monitor may give you an adequate display area. For larger audiences, you can either invest in a larger display monitor (readily available up to 33 inches) or a *data projector* which will take the images from your personal computer and project them onto a large screen. A typical projector from the Barco range is shown in Figure 5.10.

Training Applications

Slides perform a similar function to OHP transparencies, visually reinforcing and illustrating what you are saying. You might find them an attractive option if:

- you have access to a quick and convenient means of producing them
- your training courses contain substantial presentational elements that will remain the same each time you run the course
- the size of your audience means that you need to project a large image without losing its clarity
- your audience expects the quality of image, and the unobtrusive method of presentation associated with slides.

Figure 5.10 *A typical computer/video projector*

However, there are drawbacks to using slides that make slide projection less versatile as a training aid, and that can get in the way of training.

Firstly, you need blackout or near blackout conditions to see the brilliant, dense colours of slides at their best. This isn't always practical on a training course. A high intensity lamp in the slide projector will partially compensate for higher levels of light, but without the darkened room, the difference between a projected slide and an OHP transparency is much less obvious.

Secondly, the efficiency of projecting slides, which is one of its attractions, is achieved at the expense of flexibility and spontaneity. Slides are displayed in a pre-defined order, accompanied by a carefully prepared and scripted spoken commentary. This is suitable when you're talking to a large audience, because they expect just to watch and listen. But when you want to encourage your course members to think, to question and to interact with you and with each other, then the linear sequence becomes an awkward constraint.

TRAINER'S TIP

Weigh the advantages of quality of slide projection against lack of flexibility. An OHP transparency may be a better alternative.

Computer presentations

A computer-controlled presentation suffers less from these problems. The presentation software should give you the flexibility to access the different 'slides' (screen display) in whatever order you choose. Provided that you are thoroughly familiar with the contents of each slide, and construct a comprehensive menu of what is available, you can free yourself from the rigidity of keeping to a prepared sequence. You can be as spontaneous as you like in what you say, and call up whatever slides are appropriate to illustrate it.

Preparation

The slide projector

Position

When positioning a slide projector, your first concern is to project an image of the appropriate size. The larger the group, the larger the image, and therefore the further away from the screen the projector will need to be.

71

If you're using the projector in a small room, and therefore operating it yourself, you will most probably stand it at desk level, so that it won't obstruct anyone's view. Tilt it upwards to project on to the screen, and then adjust the screen angle to eliminate the keystone effect.

Light levels

Experiment with different levels of light, to see what effect they have on the quality of the image. From the course members' point of view, the more light there is, the easier it will be for them to take notes.

The computer

Position

Bear in mind that the display will be difficult to see if the sources of light in the room are reflected on the screen, or if there is a strong source of light behind the screen.

Light levels

Computer monitors have the advantage over slide projectors in that they don't need to be viewed in a darkened room.

The slides

Design principles

As with making transparencies for the OHP, your slides (or screen display, if you are using the computer as a projector) should:

- be easy to read
- project a clear message
- be memorable.

To achieve this, you should:

- severely limit the number of words or images on each slide
- use colour to achieve striking effects
- look for graphical ways of expressing information.

The overriding principle is to *keep things simple*.

Production of Materials

There are two main ways of making the 35 mm transparency needed for the slide. The first involves photographing the images required on to special film that produces a positive image, and is particularly useful if artwork or pictorial illustrations already exist.

The second method is to build up graphical images on the computer. For someone experienced in using the software, this can be a quick and easy option, with endless scope for experimentation, amendments and updating. With a digital imaging system, the computer screen can be converted into a 35 mm slide within minutes. The whole process can therefore be completed in-house, instead of involving an external production company.

Good Training Practice

Using slides effectively has much in common with good practice in using OHP transparencies. However, there are some additional points that apply only to slides.

What do you say?

You cannot preview a slide before you display it. You either rely on your notes or memory, and announce confidently what you are about to show, or else you project the slide, check that it's the one you expected, and then talk about it. If you choose the latter, there are three possible pitfalls:

1. You will give the impression that what you say is supplementary to the contents of the slide. Instead of using slides to support your input, it will seem as though they are the more important means of putting across the message.
2. You will look as though you're relying on the slide to remind you of what comes next.
3. You will turn to the screen and read from it what people would prefer to read for themselves. You will lose eye contact with them, and they will be trying to do the impossible – to listen and read at the same time.

Introducing variety

Introducing variety is a subtle process. It isn't a matter of presenting different slides in quick succession; it's more a case of varying the type of slides that you present, and pacing yourself, spending more time considering some than others. Information presented as pie charts or as a graph might warrant more attention than an illustrative picture or photograph that is supportive rather than informative.

Practicalities

As with OHP transparencies, Murphy's Law all too often comes into play. So exercise a little discipline, and number each slide according to its place in your presentation. Keep them clean, too – dust and fingerprints can ruin the effect.

Delivery

Slide presentations need very careful preparation. You might want the security of a detailed script to keep what you are saying synchronized with the sequence of slides. If this is the case, you'll have to work hard at sounding spontaneous and interesting. Any sign that you are reading from your notes is likely to reduce your credibility with your audience, and will make you more difficult to listen to.

6 Audio Equipment

▷   SUMMARY   ◁

This chapter:
- Describes the equipment needed for recording and playing audio cassettes, and for making tape-slide presentations.
- Outlines how to prepare the materials.
- Advises how the trainer can best make use of the materials on a training course.

Audio Cassettes

Audio tapes were used for many years for teaching languages, especially in language laboratories. When audio cassettes were introduced, and the cassette player became standard equipment in cars, wider possibilities suddenly appeared. New companies emerged to create new markets with managers and sales staff as prime targets. Now, although language teaching still predominates, there's a wealth of material in other fields for those seeking a more productive use of their travelling time. Listening to a 20-minute briefing tape can be more appealing than reading a book.

Trainers have the option of:

- using the pre-recorded resources on training courses
- making recordings for specific courses
- recording activities on a course.

Description of the Equipment

Tape recorders

You need look no further than your local high street for good quality audio cassette recorders. Many of them have powerful speakers, wide tonal range and two tape playing mechanisms which can be used for dubbing or copying.

Specialist models intended for education and training applications usually have multiple headphone sockets so that small groups can listen to a tape without disturbing other people in the same room. This facility may have a limited application in conventional training situations, but if you do need it, you don't necessarily have to use a recorder with the facility built in. Provided your cassette recorder has at least one headphone socket, you can connect it to a junction box and run several headphones from this.

The main consideration when choosing a recorder will probably be the quality and volume of the output. Many of the radio cassettes available in high street shops will be more than adequate in the majority of training rooms. Some now have graphic equalizers for adjusting the tone in different frequency bands. As well as a bass and treble control, they typically have three or more controls in between, so that quite subtle tone adjustments can be made to match the original recording to the acoustics of the room.

Another important feature is some form of counter that allows you to identify and get back to any part of a tape. This will usually be a mechanical counter consisting of three number wheels and a reset button.

You should also make sure that there is a socket for an external microphone if you want to make your own recordings. The built-in microphones are rarely selective enough for training applications.

Microphones and mixers

When you use a cassette recorder to record a group discussion or a role play, it's difficult to get a balanced recording with each person being heard at the same level. One way of improving the recording is to use several microphones placed around the room and plugged into a microphone mixer. You can then control the output from each microphone independently and get a more balanced result. For small groups you can give each person a small clip microphone.

Using this equipment is not as complicated as it may seem. Each microphone plugs into the mixer (you may need long leads or extensions) and a single cable connects the mixer to the microphone socket of the recorder. The mixer will most probably have its own power supply and so will also need plugging into a mains socket. The level of each microphone can then be adjusted by its own volume control. A typical set-up using a mixer is shown in Figure 6.1.

You will need to allow some time for setting up the equipment and making adjustments to the level settings, but the quality of the recording will make it worthwhile.

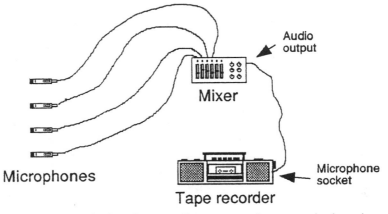

Figure 6.1 *A typical audio recording set-up using several microphones and a mixer*

Training Applications

Pre-recorded tapes

The recordings you use for training should be either commercially produced from original material, or recordings that you have produced yourself. Although there may be the occasional radio broadcast that covers a topic relevant to your subject, the copyright laws forbid you to make a recording for use in a training context. (There is, however, some relaxation of the law for certain educational broadcasts, used for educational purposes.)

If you do find commercial materials that would enhance your training, don't feel bound by their structure. Decide on what is relevant to achieving your training objectives, and use it in whatever way suits you.

Recording group activities

An alternative use for audio cassettes is for recording role-plays and discussions. If you are working with small groups, then give each group its own equipment and use it to record what they are doing. During a feedback session, either the group or a tutor could use extracts from the cassette to illustrate particular points about the role play or discussion. For something like training in telephone techniques, sound without the visual images is acceptable, and audio recordings offer a very convenient and economical alternative to using video equipment.

Preparation

Setting up audio equipment in a training situation is a straightforward process. If you decide to use a microphone mixer you should allow approximately fifteen minutes for setting up. The most important thing to check is that each microphone works. If they are battery operated, but don't seem powerful enough, try changing the batteries. Some microphones have a small switch on the side – check that this is switched on.

Production of Materials

If you decide to produce your own pre-recorded audio cassettes you will, of course, get the best sound quality if you use a professional recording engineer and a properly equipped sound studio. If you can't justify this for your application, or if it's not convenient, then you can still get good results with domestic equipment, so long as you make careful plans for when and where you record. Choose quiet surroundings and a time when you are least likely to get unwanted noise. It's not easy, because a microphone will pick up sounds that you probably won't be aware of at the time.

The professional option for producing audio cassettes may be less expensive than you imagine. Try the studios that make demo tapes for local pop groups. Their facilities may look scruffy and uninviting, but as long as they have got the equipment and a skilled engineer you should get good results.

Scripting the programme

Script-writing is an art. If you've ever tried it, you'll know how different it is from any other form of writing that you might do, and how difficult it is to create convincing dialogue. You might decide it's worth using the services of a professional script-writer, but if you take on the job yourself, the most important thing to remember is that the words will be spoken and not read. Sentence constructions that work well when they appear on the printed page may translate poorly into speech, Finding a style that sounds natural when it is spoken isn't easy. Use short, crisp sentences, and make your message clear and straightforward.

If you intend using audio simply to record various sound effects – for example, the sounds produced by different faults on an engine –

you will still need to plan the sequence of sounds and produce a written script so that you can refer to it in your training session.

You should also think carefully about the length of recording you want to make. For most applications, a few minutes of continuous talk will be quite long enough.

Enhancing the sound track

If your programme has to be more than a few minutes to cover everything you need, break up the commentary with some carefully chosen music. If you want to use commercially recorded music though, you will have to pay a copyright fee.

You can also make the programme more interesting by introducing sound effects where appropriate. These can either be recorded separately from live action and dubbed in to the final tape, or produced during the recording with a few everyday items. There is plenty of scope for using your imagination here.

Whatever you use, *keep it subtle and restrained.* If you overdo things, you'll obscure the message rather than enhance it.

Good Training Practice

Use the material to complement your training, not as a substitute for something you could equally well say yourself.

Bear in mind that when people normally listen to the radio or to a tape, they are more often than not doing something else at the same time. On a training course, they will find it difficult to concentrate solely on a disembodied voice on a tape for more than a few minutes at a time.

Tape-slide Presenters

The tape-slide presenter is the combination of the conventional slide projector with a cassette player.

Description of the Equipment

There are two main forms of tape-slide machine:

1. A conventional slide projector with a remote control socket and a special tape recorder.
2. A self-contained unit consisting of a projector, a back-projection screen and a built-in tape recorder (see Figure 6.2).

In both systems, the slide projector is controlled by a special audio track on a conventional audio cassette, which also contains the verbal presentation for a particular programme.

Figure 6.2 *A tape-slide presenter*

Using a tape-slide programme is simply a matter of loading the slides into a carousel, inserting the tape into the tape recorder and switching on. As the audio presentation begins, the appropriate slide is selected and changed automatically at a pre-programmed time by the control signals on the audio cassette.

Some models have an additional lens system for projecting the slides on to a large screen as well as on to the built-in back projection screen. So these models can be used in a similar way to a standard slide projector but with the additional advantage of a sound track.

Most models select slides in a strict linear sequence – they don't allow selection from a specified slot in the carousel (random access). So all the slides you use have to be mounted in the correct order to correspond with the audio-taped presentation. If you wanted to show a slide a second time within a presentation, you would need a second copy of it in the appropriate part of the carousel. The alternative is to choose one of the small number of models that contain a microprocessor controller, and which therefore allows you to programme a non-linear selection of slides.

Microprocessor-controlled models

The audio control track for these more sophisticated machines contains a coded signal that tells the slide projector via the microprocessor where in the carousel to find a particular slide, rather than just a pulse that tells the projector to select the next slide in the carousel. The control track in this case is actually a program that can store several types of commands. For example, one set of commands might instruct the projector to:

- move the carousel to slide number 10
- display this slide for 20 seconds
- move to slide number 34
- pause for 5 seconds
- display the slide for 15 seconds
- return to slide 10.

During this time, the audio commentary would present information appropriate to the slides being projected.

Training Applications

Tape-slide programmes can be used for individual or small group study or for a standard presentation without an experienced instructor. Since the presentation is standard, everyone receives the same basic instruction. They might also be used by an instructor to illustrate certain stages in a procedure. Where there is a single right way that must be adhered to, this is a major advantage.

TRAINER'S TIP

Tape-slide programmes could be used:
- for teaching recognition (e.g. different models of a product; layout of an instrument panel; controls on machinery that isn't easily accessible)
- for testing recognition by presenting a random series of slides (provided you have a microprocessor-controlled model)
- as a guide in real time (e.g. in an assembly task); this would be an alternative to using a manual and it could be more convenient
- as back-up instruction by offering students the opportunity to go through the package on their own, after the instructor had been through it with them
- for self-assessments by building in slides carrying test questions.

Producing a tape-slide presentation

Whichever type of tape-slide presenter you use, you will be faced with a considerable amount of preparation for each programme or presentation. The process involves:

- scripting the audio commentary
- designing and producing visuals to support the programme
- bringing the two together in a carefully planned manner, by producing a storyboard so that each slide is matched precisely with each part of the commentary
- recording the commentary, preferably in a sound studio
- adding the control track to the audio cassette.

For scripting and producing the audio tape, the same factors as for producing audio cassettes will apply, with the additional consideration of adding the control track. Slide production will be similar to the processes described in Chapter 5.

Good Training Practice

On its own, a tape-slide package is as effective as a well prepared and presented lecture, which in essence is what a tape-slide sequence is. In most situations, you are likely to use this medium as just one part of a complete training course. You will certainly need some back-up materials such as handouts for trainees to refer to.

7 Video, Film and Computers

▷   SUMMARY   ◁

This chapter:
- Provides a brief guide to different video formats and equipment.
- Outlines what is involved in producing a training video.
- Suggests different ways of using pre-recorded video tapes.
- Explains how interactive video laser discs can be used in conventional training.
- Discusses how to use video for recording and reviewing activities on training courses.

John Cleese revolutionized the ubiquitous training film. Twenty minutes of entertainment (albeit with a serious purpose) became a statutory part of every training course. But the world has moved on, and there is an ever increasing range of options to choose from, including:

- off-the-shelf videos
- bespoke productions, made either in-house or commissioned from a production company
- budget productions that you make yourself.

Then, in addition to pre-recorded material, you have the option of recording and playing back to participants the short activities that they engage in on a training course.

In this chapter, we consider what is involved in making each of these alternatives effective.

Video Recording Equipment

Description of the Equipment

You may have thought that the battle for a common format in video recording had long been won, but there is still a bewildering array of equipment that can be used for recording on to video tape. In this section we will be looking at the type of equipment you are likely to have access to for training; that used by professional video producers isn't covered.

Video recorders

When a mass market for video recorders first opened up, manufacturers built their equipment to one of several incompatible standards – either Betamax, VHS (Video Home System) or Philips/Grundig V2000 format for domestic use, or U-Matic (high or low band) for commercial and industrial applications. No recorder would play tapes recorded in a different format.

Over the years, there has been a certain amount of standardization. Currently, the most likely choice of format for pre-recorded cassettes will be VHS, which is now the standard for most domestic video equipment. It uses ½-inch tape mounted in a cassette and can be obtained in blank form with a playing duration of between 30 minutes and four hours; the most common is the three-hour tape.

If you want to use video for recording during a training session, there are other formats you may wish to consider, such as VHS-C, Video 8 and S-VHS. These are described in more detail under 'Video Cameras' below.

You might still have low band U-Matic recorders in your training department. These are cumbersome machines – heavy and awkward to move around. In the absence of pre-recorded commercial material in this format, their popularity has waned.

Television standards

If you are using pre-recorded material, one other factor you might need to consider is the difference in television standards between various parts of the world. The UK and many other western European countries have adopted PAL (Phase Alternation Line) which uses 625 lines. In France, the USSR and some eastern European countries the standard is SECAM (Séquential Couleur à Mémoire), which also uses 625 lines. But the USA, Canada, Japan and most of South America use the 525 line NTSC (American National Television Standards Committee).

If you want to use material recorded outside this country, or to send to another country material recorded here, it will need transferring to the correct national standard. This is because the different standards are incompatible – equipment designed to accept one standard cannot be used for material based on a different standard.

It is possible to get a multi-standard recorder and monitor that will handle any tape, but for most people it's more economical to get a programme transferred to the correct standard by a professional facility house.

Video cameras

For making your own video recordings – for example, of role-plays – there are yet more choices to be made. If you regularly run courses in the same place and don't need to set up the equipment every time you use it, you could use a standard VHS recorder with a separate camera. If you need something more portable, then a camcorder which has a recorder built into the camera will most probably be a better choice. This is where your options multiply.

The recorder in a camcorder will use one of the following formats: full-sized VHS; VHS-C (with cassettes that look similar to audio cassettes); Super VHS-C; Video 8, (which uses 8 mm tape); Hi 8. The VHS-C format can be played in a standard VHS recorder or playback machine using a special adaptor. However, Video 8 cassettes need a special playback machine or recorder.

A further consideration is the recorded quality that you need. If you simply want to record activities on your courses, then ordinary VHS will be adequate. However, if you want to edit your tape and make copies from it, then VHS will give you poor results. Consider instead the S-VHS (Super VHS) format which uses enhanced quality tape and recording equipment.

S-VHS machines can record in low or high band mode. (The quality of low band is more like that of VHS.) Either S-VHS or ordinary VHS tapes can be recorded in low band and played back on both S-VHS and ordinary VHS machines. S-VHS tapes can be used to record on ordinary VHS equipment, but the results will be no better than recordings made on VHS tape.

The superior quality of S-VHS is only apparent when S-VHS tape is recorded in high band on an S-VHS machine. Such recordings cannot be replayed on an ordinary VHS machine.

To help you sort out the key features associated with different video formats, they are listed in Figure 7.1.

Video format	Quality (high/ low band) *	Tapes can be played on VHS recorders?	Size/weight of camcorder
VHS	low	yes	large
VHS-C	low	yes with adaptor	small
Super VHS	high	yes if recorded in low band	large
Super VHS-C	high	yes with adaptor and recorded in low band	medium
Video 8	low	no	small
Hi 8	high	no	medium

* Quality refers to the production and editing aspects of the master tape, not to pre-recorded videos that are distributed in VHS format.

Figure 7.1 *Features of different video formats for video recorders and camcorders*

Monitors
Most of the recorders and cameras mentioned above can be connected to an ordinary television set to display the recording. With some cameras, this will involve using a special adaptor. But for most training applications you are unlikely to want to show broadcast programmes, so a video monitor is a better choice. A monitor produces a much sharper picture than a TV set because the video signal is passed directly to the electronics that produce the images on the screen rather than through an RF (radio frequency) unit on the camera or the adaptor, and then through a tuner on the television set. If you do want the option of using the monitor as a television set, then look for a model that offers both facilities.

Laser disc players
Laser disc players read still or moving video images and sound from a special disc the size of a 12-inch long-playing record. The video images

are stored on the disc as a series of frames, each of which can be accessed and displayed on a video monitor. A laser disc player could be connected to a monitor and the disc played in a linear fashion just as you would a video cassette. However, if you put the disc under the control of a computer program, then you can access the video frames in any sequence you choose. With the addition of a video overlay card, the video images can be combined with computer generated information such as text and graphics. A video overlay card is needed to combine the incompatible signals from the video laser disc and the computer. It plugs into one of the expansion slots of a PC. This is the normal set-up for interactive video used for training purposes.

Pre-recorded Video Programmes

Training Applications

Training videos have moved on from being seen simply as light relief and have been assuming a more prominent part in a training course. Several producers now offer their videos as part of a co-ordinated training strategy. Some even offer a complete training course including a trainer's manual, OHP slides, detailed case studies and student handbooks. However, both approaches tend to obscure the potential usefulness of videos as flexible training aids. If you accept that you don't necessarily have to show the whole video, and that you can extract sequences according to your particular needs, then a range of options opens up, depending on the training methods that you have chosen to use.

Consider using video to:

- provide an introduction and orientation to a particular subject
- provide good and poor models of behaviour
- draw together different threads that have already been tackled on the course
- provide self-help, perhaps when someone wants to pursue a subject that you are not covering on the course
- start a discussion
- put things into context
- provide a different stimulus or medium to learn from
- show the consequences of action (or lack of action) and behaviour that it would not be feasible to simulate
- stimulate discussion of deep rooted feelings (trigger tapes)
- quiz the trainees, e.g. 'How many examples of . . . can you spot?'

– test understanding, by providing something that can be ana-lysed in the the light of knowledge acquired on the course.

Preparation

A commercially produced video might appear to need little prepara-tion on your part, but it would be a mistake to think this. Like any other training aid you should use it only if you have a good reason for doing so; good reasons need thinking about.

If you haven't seen the video before, make sure you watch it at least twice before you use it, and read any supporting notes or resources thoroughly. If you are using one of the complete training packages that include a trainer's manual, you will need to become thoroughly familiar with the way the course is structured. Some packages encourage you to adapt the course to meet your own specific needs. If you decide to do this, allow plenty of preparation time and keep a careful note of any changes you want to make.

Before you use the video, check that:

– the equipment works
– it is in the best place for the audience to see
– you are familiar with the controls
– the video tape has been rewound to the place you want to start at (which might not necessarily be the beginning).

If you have decided to be selective about which parts of the video to show, make sure you have recorded the counter readings of the beginnings of the sequences. The best way to do this is to rewind the tape fully, reset the counter to zero, and then find the sequences you want and note the counter readings. Be sure that you do this on the machine you will actually be using – there are some surprising variations in the counter readings of different video recorders.

Good training practice

Using a training video might seem an easy option, because it's instantly attention grabbing, and usually entertaining. But your course mem-bers could lapse into a relaxed 'watching television' mode, in which case, they won't get the most out of it. So to exploit its full potential, there are various aspects of good training practice that you should bear in mind.

TRAINER'S TIP

A classroom teacher was preparing to play a video recording to her class, but couldn't get a stable video image on a television screen. This was an opportunity for some of her class to feel important and competent by showing her what to do. In these circumstances, her lack of knowledge had a very positive outcome. In the training room, though, delegates would be unimpressed by what they would see as ineptitude.

Only through thorough preparation will you be able to give a professional performance and inspire confidence in your audience.

Planning

Before you use a video, think carefully about the messages that it's putting across. Do you agree with them? Will your course members be able to identify with them? What interpretations might be made of different events? In other words, prepare yourself so that you're not taken by surprise by the comments and reactions of your course members.

Once you've decided that the video is appropriate, plan when and how you will use it.

Choose the most appropriate time and decide what you want to achieve by showing it. Then use your imagination. It's not something that you have to play through from start to finish each time you show it. If you're sufficiently familiar with it, you'll be able to control it for your own ends, rather than being tied to the design that the producer had in mind.

If you're using more than one video, space them out, to avoid overloading participants with one medium.

Showing the video

Introduce the video rather than put it on cold. Make it clear to the audience why they are being shown the video and what they should look for.

If the context of the video is different from the one in which the audience work, explain why this shouldn't make a difference to the applicability of the main messages, and that you will be discussing afterwards the extent to which the advice is transferable.

Stay in the room while the video is playing. You may have seen it too many times for comfort, but you should model the attentive behaviour that you expect from those watching it. If you leave the group, they may get the message that you are using the video as a time filler. By staying, you can observe the audience, and note their reactions; this will be useful when you come to discuss the contents.

Building on the video

Allow time to discuss and analyse the video. Relate the contents to other parts of your course, by referring to particular episodes or by basing exercises on the key points.

Alternative ways of using videos

As mentioned above, you don't need to be bound by the fact that most training videos are made as a self-contained programme, to be played from beginning to end. There are other ways of showing a video, and some producers build in a certain amount of flexibility to make it easier for the trainer to adopt alternative approaches.

For example, Longman Training's telephone training video *Who are you, by the way?* is in three sections. The first shows a caller getting poor treatment, but only his end of the conversation is shown. The second replays the conversation, but shows only the other end of the exchange. The final section gives a positive model for exemplary telephone techniques, and the benefits they can bring. The video can be stopped after the first section, and replayed for group or individual analysis of what must have been happening on the other end of the phone. This would be followed by showing the second section, and replaying it to identify all the examples of poor technique, and comparing them with the original discussion. The third section offers a similar opportunity in relation to the skilled way.

The same process of:

1. view
2. replay the section and analyse the faults
3. compare with a better model

can be used for any video that shows how not to do something, followed by a positive model.

The documentary style of *Managing pressure at work* produced by BBC Enterprises offers a different range of options. At various points, there are summaries of the key subject areas. This is an opportunity for the trainer to stop the tape, and discuss with the group how the subject matter applies to them.

This is particularly important where the video makes suggestions about good organizational practice, because without the understanding and commitment of a group of people, it would be difficult to alter

accepted practice. So a video of this type, including factual information, case studies and guidelines for good practice, can be used as the
beginning of long-term change.

Using Your Own Pre-recorded Video Programmes

Using video is not just a question of using either commercially
produced material, or recording activities during the course for
feedback purposes: a further choice is to record your own videos to
illustrate specific features. You may feel that 'home produced' videos
are not suitable for training purposes because your trainees are used to
seeing broadcast quality programmes and nothing less will do. This
isn't necessarily true. There are times when the important thing is to
show examples and procedures that are specific to your company. If
your target audience is large enough you may be able to justify using a
professional video production company, but there will be many times
when this is not an economical choice. In this case you may consider
doing it in-house. With some investment in the basic equipment, this
could be a viable option.

Description of the Equipment

Video formats

A few years ago, companies that wanted to produce their own videos
would probably have chosen low band U-Matic equipment for its good
quality reproduction and the additional facilities it could offer. This
format has lost favour over the years and the choice now is likely to be
Hi 8 or S-VHS.

The video recorders and cameras available in these formats were
described above, but there are some additional items of equipment that
will make your production more professional, and these are discussed
below.

Studio lighting

For shooting indoors, at least two studio lights will be needed: the
keylight (the main lighting source) and the fill light (for softening the
hard shadows created by the keylight). You may also find it useful to
have some coloured diffusors (*scrims*) to fit over the lights and a large
reflector to bounce the light on to the subject. These additions will help
soften the light further, if you need to. A typical arrangement for
lighting a single person is shown in Figure 7.2.

Editing equipment

You will almost certainly need to edit the tapes on which you make your

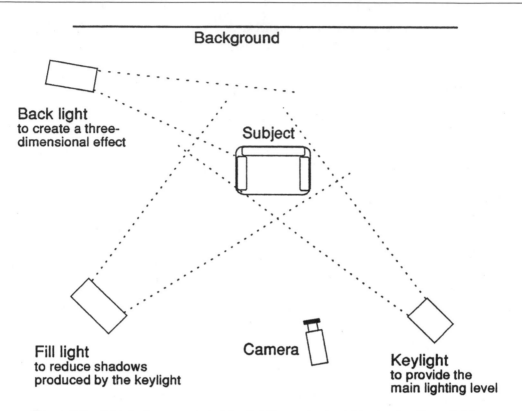

Figure 7.2 *A typical arrangement for lighting a single subject using three lights*

original recordings (what the professionals call the *rushes*). On VHS equipment, this is where the problems start to occur. Whenever you make a copy of a VHS video tape, there is a noticeable loss of picture quality, even on the first copy. The audio track also starts to suffer, although to a lesser extent. If you need to make several copies from the edited tape then the quality drops again. The colours start to fade and the images become hazy. With Hi 8 and S-VHS formats the reductions in quality are less noticeable.

Whichever format you choose, there is a range of editing equipment available that has many of the features of a professional editing suite. The basic functions of an editing machine are to control the video player (for the original tape) and the video recorder (for the edited master tape) from a single console. At the very least, it should have the facility to:

– locate accurately different parts of the rushes that you want to copy and the points in the edited master tape where you want to insert a sequence
– search forwards or backwards through the rushes at different speeds
– insert an extract from the rushes on to the edited tape, cutting in the beginning and cutting out the end cleanly and quickly at the touch of a button
– preview the sequence to be inserted before it is copied to the edited tape.

You may also want an editor that can be used with a range of different cameras or video recorders.

Whilst the final results will not be up to broadcast standard, S-VHS in particular does approach this and either this or the Hi 8 format will allow you to make a reasonable number of VHS copies from an edited tape without too much loss of visual quality.

As well as the basic editing machine, equipment is available for adding captions and graphics, and a range of special effects such as:

– colour wipes (wiping between different scenes with colours and patterns)
– split screen edits
– colour correction
– fades to black, white or a background colour.

This equipment is independent of the tape format, so you will usually have a choice of different models for your particular set-up.

Microphones and mixers

Although many cameras are fitted with a microphone (some are even 'telescopic' and will zoom in or out with the zoom lens) these are really suitable only for recording one person. If you want to record a group of people with equal clarity, then you can either use a 'boom microphone' held by an operator or use several microphones distributed around the group and a mixer. For small groups, clip microphones are easy to use and inexpensive, and give good quality sound. Several microphones can be connected to a mixer, as explained in Chapter 6.

Training Applications

The training applications for videos you produce yourself are generally the same as for commercially produced programmes. However, the main advantage in producing your own videos is that they can be specific to your company and your training objectives.

TRAINER'S TIP

For a training course on instructional skills, we needed a series of short, specially scripted vignettes to illustrate particular parts of instruction in different settings. No commercial videos would have given anything like the relevance or detail that was achieved at extremely low cost, in-house, with nothing more than good quality domestic equipment. On this occasion we used real instructors, who knew and understood the material, and who talked very convincingly.

In another example, we wrote a script for a company that wanted their own tailor-made video to support their courses on customer care, which emphasized their own house style and was obviously set within one of their branches. They couldn't justify using a professional production company, but they did employ a couple of professional actors and used the services of one of their managers who happened to be an amateur video enthusiast with a high quality domestic camera.

The results on both occasions were not commercial quality, but they fulfilled a need at a very modest cost and were both totally accepted by their different audiences. The alternative would have been no video at all.

Production of Materials

If you do decide to use professional expertise, you will need to prepare a comprehensive brief and choose a company that can produce a video that will meet your needs. These tasks can be quite time consuming, but are worth doing thoroughly because mistakes at this planning stage can have expensive consequences.

Preparing a brief

Before you approach a production company you must be:

- sure that a video is an appropriate response to a training need
- clear about what you want the video to achieve.

You should also have considered:

- specific training objectives that need to be covered – do they relate to knowledge, attitudes or specific behaviour?
- the target audience – who is it mainly aimed at? Is there a range?
- the length of the video – this may be dictated by what you need to cover
- the programme style – do you have any strong reasons for: drama, presenter with short action sequences, documentary, trigger sequences?
- your involvement – are you the main client, i.e. the person who can make the decisions? Which parts of the production process do you want to be involved in?

- which parts of the process you want the production company to handle – some companies would expect to take a brief from the client and organize the whole process from scripting to editing and post production; others may be more flexible and willing to work with your own personnel
- the size of your budget – this will affect some of the other factors such as style of video, type of actors or presenter you want to use and the overall length of the video.

Choosing a video company

Video production companies abound. They come in all shapes and sizes from the single producer/director/script-writer working with freelance help, to well established production houses with every function represented on the permanent staff. But size is not the main criterion for your choice. Track record in the kind of video you want is a much more reliable guide.

Since you are more likely to want a training video rather than a marketing video or a corporate video, this will narrow your choice. Try to get a recommendation from someone whose judgement you trust and then approach no more than two or three companies with a detailed brief. If they are worth using, they should be willing to work on a few outlines from your brief, without charge. They should also be willing to show you examples of the work they have produced for other clients.

'If you don't know where you're going, you'll end up somewhere else' is so true of video production, where anything is possible but at a price. If you've got a strict budget to work within, get the video company to make a commitment about what they will do for an agreed amount. Check that this will meet your training objectives. Then see that both you and they stick to the agreement.

Producing your own video

Although you may decide to undertake all aspects of the production process in-house, you will still need to prepare a brief and consider the issues listed above. In addition you will need to decide whether to use any professional services for some parts of the process. For example, you may decide to use a professional script-writer and professional actors or a presenter.

The detailed aspects of producing a video are beyond the scope of this book, but there are some excellent guides you can consult. These are listed in the further reading section at the back of the book.

Good Training Practice

Using a video you have produced yourself is no different from using a commercial product, with the exception of one produced 'in-house'. Before you show a 'home made' video to your audience, you should warn them that what they are about to see is not commercially produced, otherwise they may waste time criticizing the production standards, rather than concentrating on the content.

Using Video to Record Course Members

The Recording Equipment

The equipment you would use for recording course members is likely to be chosen from the list given earlier in this chapter. But since you are unlikely to want to copy or edit the recording, you won't really need the higher quality offered by Hi 8 and S-VHS. Your choice is more likely to be between VHS (normal or C format tapes) or standard 8 mm. A camcorder, rather than a separate video recorder, will cut down on the amount of equipment you need, and the camera will be smaller and more portable.

Training Applications

The most likely reasons for making impromptu recordings during a course are to:

- record role-plays, etc. so that subsequent discussion is based on what actually happened, rather than on participants' and observers' memories (incidentally, this can demonstrate how much is missed or ignored at the time it happens)
- provide individuals with a permanent record of what they have done, to which they can refer later
- record yourself, so that you can see whether there are aspects of your performance that you want to improve
- record aspects of skilled/unskilled performance (psychomotor skills) and then to replay using the pause or slow motion facilities to highlight aspects that otherwise happen too fast to be observed.

Preparation

The technically minded will be happy to spend time checking the equipment, but then ignore the need to talk through with the participants what is expected of them. The more people-orientated trainers may be tempted to take the equipment for granted, but then find themselves in an embarrassing situation when they can't make it work.

Preparation means taking nothing for granted, so check your equipment thoroughly, and allocate time on the course to discuss the recording process with your participants.

Preparing the equipment

Your priority here is to make sure it works. Yes, it's obvious, but there's no guarantee that what worked yesterday or last week is still working today. Some of the most common reasons for video equipment not working are:

- faulty leads, usually damaged by careless handling
- discharged batteries in camcorders and microphones
- operator error in making a recording.

Keep the equipment manuals handy, especially if your participants will be making their own recordings.

Once you are satisfied that the equipment works, check next that it is in a suitable position. The overriding consideration here is that the camera shouldn't be directed towards the main source of light. If you need to use daylight, point the camera away from a window. If you are using studio lights, place them either side of the camera and directed towards the subjects to get the best all round lighting with even shadows.

You may have the option of a room separate from the training room in which to do the recording. The main advantages of this arrangement are that the equipment can be set up in advance and left, and participants are less aware of the audience watching them. However, there are drawbacks. It means that you cannot control things as easily as if the recording is done in the training room and the constant switching between rooms makes it impractical to record and then discuss very short parts of an activity.

TRAINER'S TIP

A trainer was running her first course for a training consultancy, and using the video recorder to record group activities. The process continued after lunch, but she was dismayed to find that the first recording of the afternoon had picked up the sound only.

What had happened was that during the break, the company administrator had been in and replaced the lens cap, in the mistaken belief that the lens would be damaged if left uncapped. The trainer hadn't noticed this, and so recorded no picture. The moral of the story is: always check the equipment before using it.

Preparing your participants

Among any group of people on a training course you will find a mixture of reactions to appearing on a video. Some can't wait to show what stars they are, some will be quite indifferent and a few may be fearful. If you are satisfied that you have a good reason for using video equipment then you should be able to allay the fears of the minority if you:

- reassure them about appearing on video
- don't try to coerce someone who genuinely does not want to participate; you may find they change their mind when they have seen others on video
- don't make too much of an issue of it
- explain that the recording will not be seen by anyone outside the course and that all tapes will be wiped clean. If participants have a tape of their own, check that anyone else appearing on it in any role has no objection to the tape being retained and replayed by the holder.

Good Training Practice

Few people fail to learn something from seeing themselves on a video recording. To maximize the benefit, you need to discipline yourself to record carefully and play back selectively and sensitively.

Making the recording

First decide what you want to record. This is not necessarily the simple decision that it might seem. Take, as an example, a training course on selection interviewing. It can be helpful to participants to practise small parts of the process first, or particular skills, so you would record just a few minutes at a time. This gives each participant some experience of performing in front of the camera while doing a task that isn't too demanding. You would then move on to longer exercises and therefore longer recordings.

It's usually adequate to focus the camera on the participants in a particular exercise and leave it in the same position throughout. You need to devote all your attention to keeping track of what is going on and making your notes so that you can guide the feedback in a helpful and structured way. Zooming in and out is unlikely to help the subsequent discussion unless the purpose of an exercise is to focus on detailed reactions.

When you have a group to video, try to get as far back as possible or else use a wide angled lens. Trying to record a group discussion in which the participants are huddled together just so that they can all get in the picture doesn't make it easy for them to act naturally.

If you do move the camera back, check what happens to the sound levels. If the microphone is an integral part of the camera, you could find that it can't pick up the conversation.

Playing back

Only for very short recordings will you be able to play back from start to finish. For anything longer, you will have to be selective. If you note counter readings at significant points as the recording progresses, and make notes about what was happening at the time, you can quickly locate the parts that are most appropriate to replay.

Be tactful in your feedback. You may find that certain participants will disassociate themselves from their performance, saying 'It was an artificial situation. I'm not like that in reality.' In this case, you might have to probe gently to find out what made them behave atypically, or concentrate on specific parts of the video (but not just the worst bits) and discuss with the individual what they were thinking and feeling at the time.

Try to involve other members of the group in the feedback, but make sure that they are fair and balanced. Encourage specific, constructive comments, rather than global judgements about whether something was good or bad. If you suggest in advance, specific aspects of performance to look for and give feedback on, then the quality is likely to be better than if they have had no structure.

Film

Film has generally been superceded by video, though some video companies still supply certain titles on 16 mm film. Some organizations too, might still have a library of films that they continue to use.

Potentially, the uses of film are similar to those for video, but film projectors lack the convenience of video player features such as frame pause, fast forward and reverse, and slow play.

The advantage of film is that it can be shown to a large audience because of the size of image that can be projected. However, video projectors are now available (see above) that offer the same size advantage, and give high definition without the need to darken the room. The main drawback of these projectors is their comparatively high cost.

TRAINER'S TIP

If you have access to a library of films that are still useful, then consider having them transferred on to video tape. The costs are modest and the extra convenience and flexibility are considerable.

Extending the use of IV Laser Discs

Interactive video (IV) is normally designed with self-study in mind, but much of the material on the laser disc used in IV could be used by trainers with a group of students. There are now IV discs containing numerous short, high quality video sequences that are ideal for illustrating a training point. This is especially true in the area of interpersonal skills such as negotiating, assertiveness, sales techniques and many more.

IV has the advantage over video cassettes in that any frame on a laser disc can be accessed almost instantly, and with great accuracy. However, access has been programmed according to the needs of the learner working step-by-step through the courseware. Until recently, the only other ways to access precise sequences on a laser disc were by using a programming language, an authoring system such as TenCore or the commands built into video board control software such as the MIC system software.

However, for trainers who want to show extracts from the discs, there is now a convenient alternative. A piece of computer software called PC Opensoft offers a straightforward way of identifying, calling up and controlling any number of extracts.

With only a limited knowledge of computing, most trainers will be able to produce professional presentations, ranging from a simple linear format to complex branching programmes in which selections can be made from a series of menus, icons or parts of the video picture, by clicking on the appropriate area of the screen with a mouse.

The software consists of three parts:

- *Designsoft*, which is used to create, edit and test the presentation. It contains facilities to draw graphics and enter text overlaid on the video image, and to create a series of 'pages' (screens of video or computer graphics or a mixture of both) that can be linked in various ways.
- *Presentsoft*, which presents and controls the sequences and timing in a presentation.
- *Searchsoft*, which can search and log sequences or frames on the video disc for access later using a keyword facility.

A set of tools is available in each part of the software, including the facility to play the video disc forwards or backwards at normal, slow and fast speeds, to scan the disc or even go to a specific frame number.

EXAMPLE: MENU SYSTEM

Figure 7.3 shows an example of a simple menu system designed to access video sequences from the Longman Training's *An Introduction to Assertiveness*. The main menu (Figure 7.3(a)) gives access to seven sub-menus. Clicking with the mouse on the first item 'What would you do?', brings up a sub-menu (Figure 7.3(b)) that gives access to 15 short scenarios illustrating different contexts where the skills of assertiveness could be used. Clicking on one of these items will call up the sequence, play it through and pause. Clicking anywhere in the centre of the screen returns the trainer to the sub-menu.

The trainer can return to the main menu by clicking in the box at the bottom right of the screen and then select another sub-menu. Alternatively, clicking on the small box containing an 'M' at the top left of the screen produces another menu that allows a short-cut means of moving around the presentation.

Figure 7.4 illustrates a more complex example of using PC Opensoft, and is again taken from Longman Training's *An Introduction to Assertiveness*.

Figure 7.4(a) is a stilled frame, showing the various characters in an office meeting. Areas of the screen around each person in the group have been defined. Clicking within an area calls up a sequence appropriate to that person. In this case, it depicts what the individual is thinking about a manager's presentation.

As a further refinement, the names of each main character and a title have also been added as text boxes overlaid on to the video still.

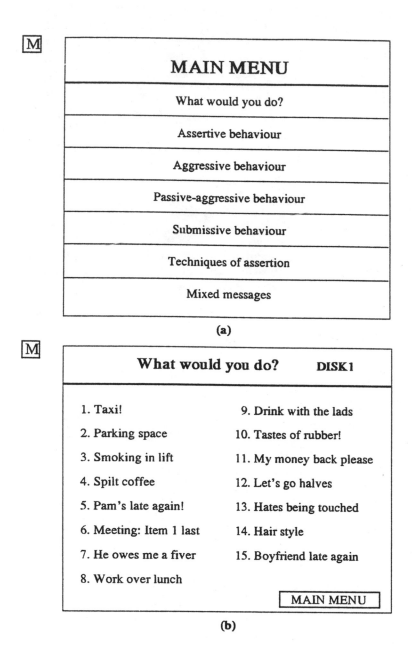

Figure 7.3 *Menus produced by PC Opensoft to access video sequences from Longman Training's IV package: 'An Introduction to Assertiveness'*

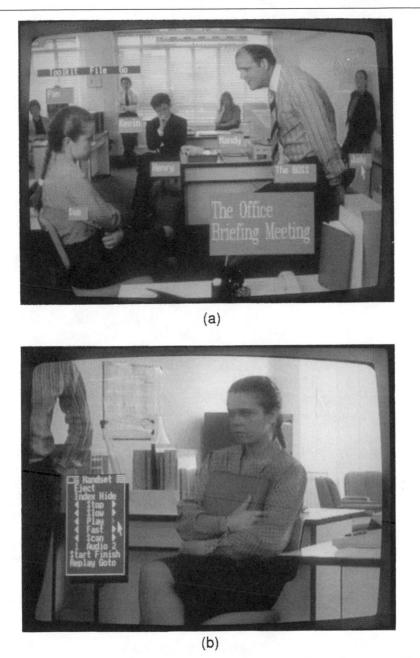

(a)

(b)

Figure 7.4 *Using PC Opensoft to access video sequences from Longman Training's* An Introduction to Assertiveness. *The titles and name plates were added from the software. (b) shows a scene accessed by clicking on Sue in the stilled frame (a).*

Using existing IV programmes in this way opens up a new and flexible resource for trainers. If you choose to exploit it, the major practical consideration in the training room will be how you display the video images. For small groups (up to six participants) a standard IV station with a 14-inch monitor will be sufficient for the presentation. For larger groups, consider using a larger monitor or a large screen projector, such as those described in Chapter 5.

Using Computers for Training in Computer Applications

As already mentioned, a computer can be used as an alternative to the OHP in projecting slides. But computers are used extensively as the main training aid in all forms of training in the use of computer applications. Applications include spreadsheets, word processing, databases and desk-top publishing as well as technical training for programmers and technical specialists in software development and advanced uses of hardware.

Description of the Equipment

For most applications the equipment is likely to be a stand-alone IBM or compatible computer. This equipment is described in Chapter 10. However, it is likely that the trainer will have a similar set-up to the students with the addition of a large monitor or a data projector. There may be occasions when the computers are networked, i.e. linked to each other and to the tutor's machine. This is dealt with in more detail in Chapter 10.

Preparation

However long you think you may need to set up several sets of computer equipment and get it all working smoothly – double it! If there was ever a case for proving Murphy's Law, using several computers on a training course will give you ample opportunity to do just that.

> ## TRAINER'S TIP
>
> Don't assume that because your equipment was all working perfectly when you left it at night, it will still be fine the following day. Who knows what gremlins will have been at work, so again, be generous with your setting up time *every day*.

Production of Materials

If your course aims are to teach people how to use an application such as a spreadsheet, most of the material you will use will have been produced by the software house. However, you may want to devise some specific exercises that illustrate the various facilities of the computer package. Producing these exercises will normally be possible within the application. However, on rare occasions, you may need to use a programming language to produce a particular effect. If you are not adept at writing programs yourself, get a programmer to produce it for you.

Good Training Practice

Many of the points already made for the use of audio-visual aids apply equally to using computers. But there is the additional fact that by sitting your students at a computer, you expect them to be doing something for much of the time, not sitting there listening to you. Keep your talk short and to the point, or they will stop listening and begin experimenting for themselves.

Planning a course that involves students in 'hands-on' learning, does need very careful thought. For much of the time they will all be at different stages of working through the exercises. During these periods it will be difficult to stop the more advanced students racing ahead, while you concentrate on those who need your help. You have to be prepared to live with this, because the alternative involves enforcing restrictions that your students may resent.

8 Job Aids and Fault Museums

▷   SUMMARY   ◁

This chapter:
- Outlines different types of job aid.
- Discusses how job aids can be used as training aids with particular reference to producing and using fault museums.

Industrial trainers are well aware of the power of using real equipment (rather than diagrams or even simulations) to explain the working or use of machinery, particularly for assembly tasks, maintenance procedures and operational tasks. In this chapter, we look at the training aids that are useful to back up training on the actual equipment.

Job Aids

In many cases, training aids are synonymous with job aids, which give trainees an overview of what is involved in an assembly task or a procedure, as well as the details needed for learning the job. The aids therefore have a dual function: to the novice, they are a training aid; to the more experienced worker, they are a job aid that serves as a check or a memory jogger.

Forms of Job Aids

Job aids come in many forms, some of which are outlined below.

Charts

These are commonly used to show components and the sequence in which they are assembled in an assembly task. They are often drawn in the form of an exploded diagram and pinned up near a workbench. Where there are several models of a product with only marginal differences, these differences would be highlighted in the diagram.

Checklists

The sequence of steps in a procedure – e.g. loading a word processor, or sending an invoice – are frequently drawn up as a checklist. In some cases, these steps can be actually checked off as they are completed; for example, the list of maintenance checks in a vehicle servicing schedule, or the pre-flight checks conducted by airline pilots. They are useful in training to reduce the memory load or, for more experienced personnel, they act as a reminder.

Maintenance manuals

Workshop maintenance manuals usually include disassembly and re-assembly procedures as well as fault-finding charts. Many of these charts, circuit diagrams and exploded views would be impossible to memorize, so for most technicians, mechanics and service engineers, they are an essential part of their toolkit.

Posters

Posters showing exploded or cut-away views of equipment are typically used in workshops and technical training centres as a permanent reference for students. They do have drawbacks, though, because they can be expensive to produce, and once they have been in place for some time, they tend to be ignored.

Keyboard overlay cards

Most computer applications such as word processors, databases and spreadsheets use numerous commands that have to be memorized. A special card listing some or all of these commands is often placed over the keyboard to act as a reminder, both while learning to use the application and as a more permanent aide-mémoire. They are especially useful if the function keys have been programmed, for example, F1 = Save and resume, F2 = Erase word, etc. A typical overlay card that fits over part of a computer keyboard is shown in Figure 8.1. Some computer applications have incorporated these features into their screen layout and display them at the bottom of the screen.

Use of colour coding

Colour codes are sometimes used to help trainees learning to use

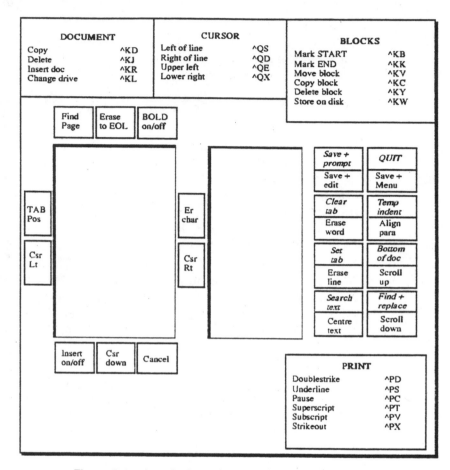

Figure 8.1 *A typical overlay card for a word processor*

equipment. Marking a typewriter or computer keyboard is an example: the left-hand keys could be marked with red self-adhesive dots and the right-hand keys with green, while the home keys could be marked with two dots in their appropriate colour.

Colour coding can be extended to various machines where the controls that can be operated or adjusted by the operator are marked in one colour, and those that must not, in another. If there is a particular order in which the adjustments or operations must be carried out, these could be numbered. The large range of stick-on labels found in stationers are ideal for this job.

Flashcards

Flashcards are regularly used in primary schools, but this shouldn't obscure their value in helping adults to memorize things that seem to have no logical structure.

A typical example is the international code signal flags use at sea. Each flag represents either a letter of the alphabet, a number or a standard message. Some illustrations are shown in Figure 8.2. In this example, the tutor would take a very small sample of flags, and explain what each one means. The trainees will then be shown an individual card taken randomly from the sample, and asked to identify it. This is repeated several times, and again in later sessions with an extended sample of cards. This reinforces what has already been learned while at the same time adding new items, until eventually, the entire range of items will have been covered.

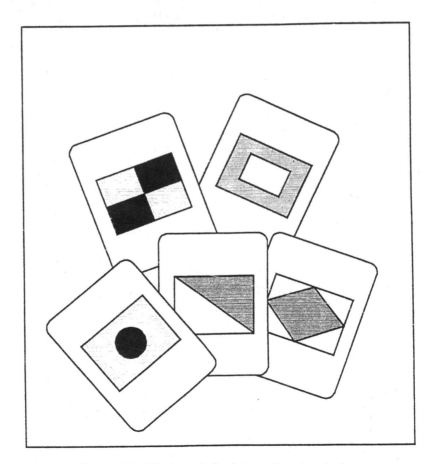

Figure 8.2 *Flash cards for international code flags*

For further reinforcement, each student could be given their own set of cards, so that they can continue learning on their own or in pairs whenever they have a few moments to spare.

The same approach can be used with international road signs, vocabulary in a foreign language or product knowledge of different models of a product.

Training Applications

Training aids can be given to trainees as part of their course notes and used on the course. They will become a job aid, and continue in use for as long as is necessary, once the trainee starts doing the job.

But not all job aids emanate from training courses. The charts that help people operate the modern multi-functional photocopiers are excellent examples of job aids made available to the widest possible audience. They help people to learn for themselves, without needing the intervention of a formal training programme.

Producing Job Aids

Decisions about who produces job aids depends on the nature of the aid and what purpose it has to serve. Some job aids are clearly best left to specialist producers. Workshop manuals to be used by experienced personnel as well as trainees are an example. But there are many other aids that can easily be produced by the trainer.

For example, for simple checklists, all you need is a wordprocessor (preferably one with the facility to draw lines and create boxes). If you have some basic artistic skills, you can draw up assembly charts. Alternatively, photocopy the relevant parts of the components catalogue, and add appropriate captions or instructions.

Keyboard overlay cards are not difficult to make, either, and by doing them yourself you can include what you know will be useful, not what the software programmer thought would be needed.

TRAINER'S TIP

Your starting point, as always, is to consider what will be most effective in helping trainees to achieve the training objectives. If a job aid exists already that perfectly fits the bill, then use it. But if existing resources cannot easily be modified to help you in your task, then consider producing your own.

Fault Museums

A fault museum is a form of job aid that is used to help trainees learn discrimination skills in achieving acceptable levels of quality in their job. These perceptual skills may involve any of the senses depending on the task, but they will usually be of a visual nature. A fault museum consists of a graded set of products (or parts of them) with a range of different faults in them. The 'museum' should also contain an example that is of an acceptable quality standard so that the trainee has a reference point.

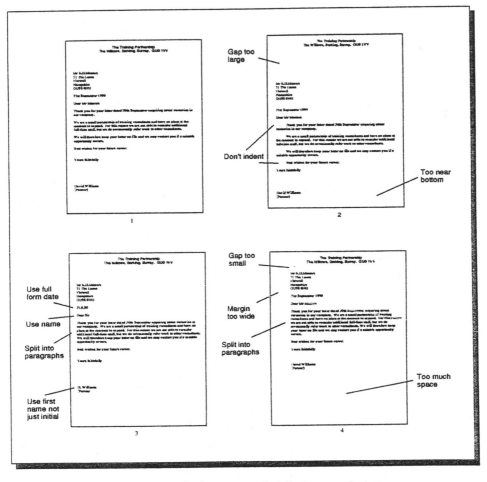

Figure 8.3 *A fault museum for the layout of a letter*

An example used for letter writing is shown in Figure 8.3. Here, the contents of a letter are shown in four different forms, three with a different set of faults and one that is of an acceptable standard. This particular example shows the four samples mounted on a board and includes captions to indicate specific faults.

Training Applications

Fault museums can be used for training in all parts of a production process and for inspection of finished products. 'Production' is not restricted to manufacturing – it could refer to processes as diverse as producing artwork, writing reports, making garments and laying bricks.

The purpose of using a fault museum is to develop in trainees an awareness of:

- quality standards that are appropriate at a particular stage of production
- the need to maintain quality standards throughout the production process instead of relying on a final inspection to identify faults.

The example in Figure 8.3 used captions. Some trainers may prefer to use unmarked samples and get the trainees to identify the faults for themselves. In this form, the fault museum can be used during training and as a test after training. If you use samples from a fault museum in this way, choose different examples for training and for testing, otherwise you will be testing the trainees' memories rather than their ability to discriminate.

A fault museum with captions showing the most common faults often provides a useful reminder to recently qualified personnel. Mounted near their normal place of work, it can act as a convenient aide-mémoire until they have fully developed their skills.

Producing a Fault Museum

A fault museum is best produced by trainers. All that is needed is a set of products with a known and varied set of faults built into them and some separate record of which specimen contains which faults.

The specimens you produce should be sufficiently different in quality standards to allow the trainees to detect what the differences are. In the letter writing example we have given this is easy, but with some tasks the differences in quality standards may be hard to detect. In these cases you may need several sets of examples of varying degrees of difficulty, so that the least experienced trainees would be asked to make less subtle discriminations than would be expected from their more experienced colleagues.

You may even want to include examples that are of a higher sta·dard than you would normally expect, so that trainees learn to distinguish between what is acceptable, and what is near-perfect but not cost-effective in terms of the time and effort needed to achieve it. Recognizing this cut-off point is an important characteristic of experienced and productive workers.

9 Course Documentation

┌───┐

▷   SUMMARY   ◁

This chapter:
- Describes different types of course documentation.
- Discusses how each type can be used to reinforce learning.

└───┘

'Course documentation? Oh, you mean handouts.' Well, yes, we do mean handouts, but not *just* handouts, and certainly not the usual sort of handouts that are distributed almost as an optional extra. What we mean by course documentation is a range of paper-based material that underpins your effectiveness as a trainer and helps participants to learn from your training courses.

Description and Training Applications

In previous chapters, various pieces of equipment were described before their training applications were discussed. With course documentation, there's no hardware involved and, as the contents are what matter, the description of each document has been combined with a discussion of how you can use it.

Different Types of Documentation

Handouts for Summarizing your Inputs

A traditional handout provides a brief review of the contents of what the trainer has said. Its purpose is to give participants a permanent and accurate record to take away, and to free them from the need to take copious notes.

So far, so good, but do they ever get read? Most probably not, because they tend to be distributed at the end of a session on the basis of 'This gives you a summary of what we've been talking about' and not referred to again. You can be fairly sure that the course folder will quickly be consigned to the bottom of a drawer and all the work you put into producing informative and comprehensive handouts will be wasted.

It doesn't have to be like this. There are ways of designing handouts that will be referred to and actively used during a training session, but which still fulfil the function of providing essential information. The key is to make them interactive.

Interactive Handouts

First, consider this question: When you are giving a short input on a course – talking for perhaps 15–20 minutes – what are the course members doing? 'Listening' no doubt, but what else? Are they copying what you have written on the flipchart, or getting down as much as they can about what you have said? Maybe they are doodling, looking out of the window or just day dreaming. How much of the time are they *actively processing* what they hear?

These are important questions. Even if your audience is apparently paying attention to you – listening and taking notes – they are not necessarily mentally active. They may be simply 'hearing' what you say, without questioning it, applying it to themselves or deciding whether it is important or not. Similarly, taking notes may mean that they are doing nothing more than recording your words. In either case, they are not getting as much out of the session as they could.

An interactive handout would involve them in doing something that made them think. Instead of being simply a narrative, it would have plenty of blank spaces for participants' contributions. It would include questions to:

- get participants thinking about their own experiences of the topic under consideration
- test their level of knowledge

        – check their understanding of what has already been covered
        – ask how they could apply new information
        – identify problems that could arise.

You would pose such questions as appropriate, as part of your input; allow participants time to consider and note their answers; and finally discuss what they thought. The answers might already be printed at the top of the next page (tell your group not to read ahead, or else distribute the pages one at a time), but the point is that each person in your group will have been prompted into something more mentally active than just listening or copying.

The handout is not merely for asking questions. The questions, or any other activities that might be appropriate, will appear among section headings, summaries, key information and anything else that you want participants to consider.

TRAINER'S TIP

The key difference between traditional and interactive handouts is that the former are 'take-aways' for future reference. The latter stimulate active involvement during the course. This means that participants concentrate harder. You find out more about them and whether they are understanding what you are saying, and they have the opportunity to sort out any misunderstandings or lack of clarity.

As well as this, interactive handouts retain the advantages of the more conventional versions, by providing accurate information and lightening the burden of notetaking. Because participants have contributed to them, they will identify them as their own.

Quizzes

Trainers are sometimes faced with the problem of judging the level at which to pitch their training. Even with in-house courses, it isn't always possible to ensure that every course member is starting at roughly the same level. If you assume too little knowledge, they will feel you are talking down to them. If you assume too much, some of them will be left behind.

One way of getting round this is to conduct an informal paper-based quiz near the beginning of your course. The results of this will give you some indication of where to start.

There's an added benefit in that it helps participants to assess their state of knowledge. For those who might have been tempted to overestimate it, this can be a useful start to the course.

Briefing Notes for Activities

You announce an activity and give the instructions for it; then you allocate participants into groups, and rearrange the room to accommodate the different groups; finally, you tell them to start. What happens? As each group settles down to work, the discussions begin about what they are expected to do. If you simply gave spoken instructions, and then spent time on the physical arrangements, the chances are that people will have forgotten much of what you said. A state of confusion is no way to get an activity off to a good start, so you need some good briefing notes.

When you prepare them, think about both the contents and the layout, because participants need to be able to extract the relevant information quickly and easily.

Firstly, give a brief outline of the purpose of the activity. This gives people an initial overview, so that they can see where they are going. Once this has been made clear, you can move into more detail about specific details – rules, constraints, assumptions, background information, etc.

Display the information clearly, with plenty of headings to break it up, and white space in between each section. Use bullet points to highlight information that would otherwise get embedded in text. When course members are using the briefing notes, they don't want to spend time reading through paragraph after paragraph, just to find the single piece of information they need.

It's helpful, too, to keep information about running the activity (objectives, timing, allocating roles, etc.) separate from the background information that will be used in the activity.

Figures 9.1 and 9.2 show different ways of presenting the background information to be used by one party in a negotiating exercise. The narrative form of the first version makes it difficult to extract information. The second version reflects the way the information will be used in the activity, and is therefore much easier to read and to refer to.

Self-Assessment Sheets

If your courses are about developing skills, then no doubt you will be giving participants plenty of individual feedback after their practice sessions. Take as an example, a course on selection interviewing. After

Estate Agent's brief

You are Miss Quickdeal, a negotiator for Trustworthy and Co. Estate Agents. You have only been with them for a year and your sales for the last three months are down. Although you wouldn't willingly admit it, you're getting anxious and desperately need some good sales very quickly.

You know that you can sell houses, and you are confident that you are good at valuations. Unofficially, you have valued properties which have been sold by your colleagues and you have usually estimated the selling price very accurately. The problem is that you always seem to get the houses which are difficult to sell - and you're not even getting many of those, at the moment.

The latest property allocated to you belongs to Mr and Mrs Housego. It's a three bedroomed detached Victorian house which has been on the books of another agent. The Housegos have asked your company for a valuation.

You know the area very well. It's not particularly popular with buyers, nor do you feel very positive about it. Despite the attractiveness of the houses, you know that they are not easy to sell. However, if you sound pessimistic to the Housegos, they might not want to use your services.

You have been informed (from reliable sources) that the house is overpriced, but you don't yet know what the vendors want for it.

You also suspect that other agents have been asked to value the property. In your experience, most vendors instruct the agent who gives the highest valuation. This makes you wary about being completely open with the Housegos about what you think their house will fetch, even though you know that your valuation will be realistic.

You want the business. You will stress that your company stays open later than other agencies in the area, which means more prospective purchasers looking at the properties on its books.

Based on your knowledge of houses in the area, you are prepared to say that an asking price of £79,950 is possible, but that £74,950 would attract more interest and produce a quicker sale. Privately, you think that the house would sell for around £72,000.

What you are trying to do is convince the Housegos that you will get them a buyer very quickly at a fair price, if they accept your valuation.

© The Hamelin Partnership 1987

mander roleplay #2

Figure 9.1 *Background information for a negotiation exercise*

HOUSE SALE

Estate Agent's Brief

Background

You are Miss Quickdeal, a negotiator for Trustworthy and Co. Estate Agents. You have only been with them for a year and your sales for the last three months are down. Although you wouldn't willingly admit it, you're getting anxious and desperately need some good sales very quickly.

You know that you can sell houses, and you are confident that you are good at valuations. Unofficially, you have valued properties which have been sold by your colleagues and you have usually estimated the selling price very accurately. The problem is that you always seem to get the houses which are difficult to sell - and you're not even getting many of those, at the moment.

The Housegos' Home

The latest property allocated to you belongs to Mr and Mrs Housego. It's a three bedroomed detached Victorian house which has been on the books of another agent. The Housegos have asked your company for a valuation.

You know the area very well. It's not particularly popular with buyers, nor do you feel very positive about it. Despite the attractiveness of the houses, you know that they are not easy to sell. However, if you sound pessimistic to the Housegos, they might not want to use your services.

You have been informed (from reliable sources) that the house is overpriced, but you don't yet know what the vendors want for it.

You also suspect that other agents have been asked to value the property. In your experience, most vendors instruct the agent who gives the highest valuation. This makes you wary about being completely open with the Housegos about what you think their house will fetch, even though you know that your valuation will be realistic.

What you are trying to do is convince the Housegos that you will get them a buyer very quickly at a fair price, if they accept your valuation.

Keyfacts - Public info

You are quite happy to reveal the following information:

- You are a good negotiator and very accurate at valuation.

- You are prepared to say that a price of £79,950 is reasonable but they will get a quicker sale if they ask £74,950.

- You stay open later than most estate agents in the area, so you can see more prospective buyers during week days.

Keyfacts - Private info

You are anxious not to reveal the following information, unless the Housegos persuade you to by asking the right questions:

- You need sales, urgently.

- This is not your kind of area and although you like the house, you know it won't be easy to sell.

- You have a poor sales record for the last three months, and very little is being offered to you at the moment.

- In your opinion the Housegos' house would be more realistically priced at £72,000

- You might accept a joint agency with a share of the commission.

• The Hamelin Partnership 1987

MANDEV ROLEPLAY #2

Figure 9.2 *Background information for negotiation exercise. The information from Fig 9.1 presented in a more accessible format using desktop publishing software.*

appropriate input and discussion, the first activity concerns the opening of the interview – welcoming the candidate, a few pleasantries, an outline of how the interview will be structured, etc. Each member of the course practises this first stage and receives feedback on their performance. When this has finished, the trainer and course member jointly summarize the most important points, and the latter notes them down on a self-assessment form. (An example is shown in Figure 9.3). Each person completes one every time they participate in an activity.

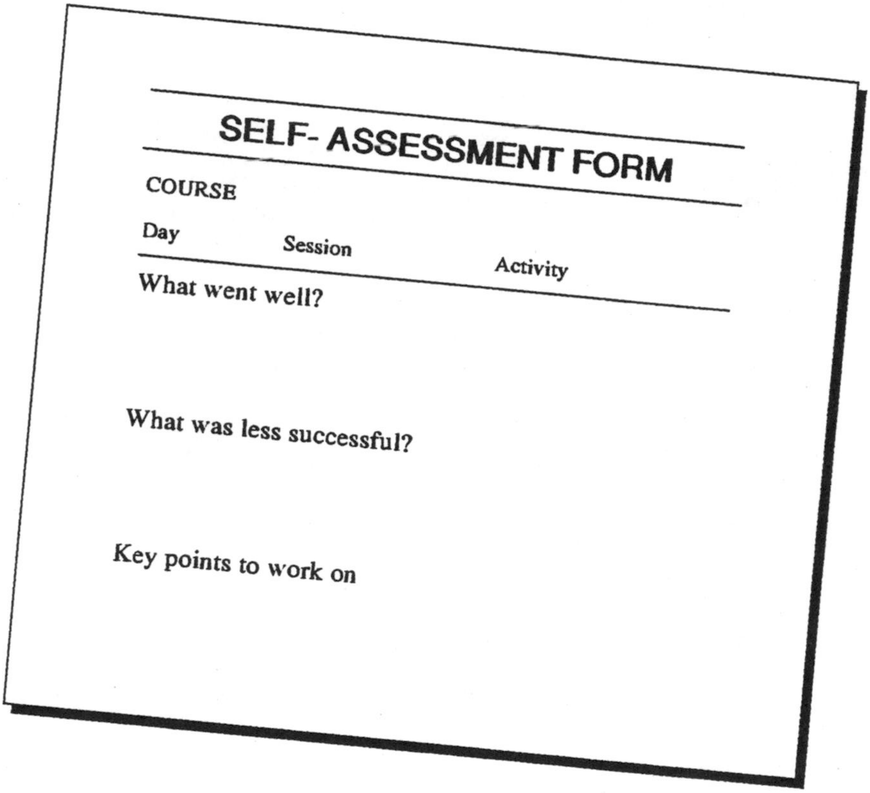

SELF-ASSESSMENT FORM

COURSE

Day   Session   Activity

What went well?

What was less successful?

Key points to work on

Figure 9.3   *A simple self-assessment form for activities*

Action Plans

Action plans are not so much a means of getting your training message across – more a way of bridging the gap between the course and the job. Don't just give course members a blank sheet of paper and ask them to write a few notes. Instead, encourage them to be specific. Provide them with an outline that makes them think about actual situations in which they will try to apply their new skills or knowledge. One possible format is given in Figure 9.4.

Figure 9.4 *A Post-course action planning sheet*

Participants' Workbooks

Most people who have been on a course come away with an untidy folder stuffed with a mixture of course handouts, notes, doodles, and illegible scraps of paper that have no significance.

An alternative is to put together a participants' workbook. This could still be in looseleaf format, but would provide a well ordered, comprehensive record of the contents of the course. It could include:

- copies of every OHP transparency or flipchart that was prepared in advance; this means that your course members don't struggle to copy what you display
- handouts that are a summary of your input
- interactive handouts to encourage active involvement in your input sessions
- details of the instructions for any activities (such as role-plays)
- self-assessment forms
- feedback sheets for particular activities, with indications of what to look out for
- blank sheets of paper for notes.

TRAINER'S TIP

The advantage of keeping to a loose leaf format for participants' workbooks is that you can control when you distribute the contents. Your course members won't be distracting you by jumping ahead to later parts of the course. It also means that you give out the documentation relating only to what you cover. If you decide that certain parts of your course aren't needed, then you simply hold back the documentation.

Preparation

Training department archives are full of unidentified handouts, many of them containing possibly useful material, but with no indication of who devised them and for what purpose. So when you are preparing course documentation, include on each sheet:

- the course for which they were designed
- a subject heading
- date of production
- your initials.

Users will benefit from this too, particularly if they refer to the material some time after the course.

If you have the contents stored on disk, then it would be easy to add the date to the title of the course, each time you copy a batch for a particular event. This is a small touch, but one that makes users feel that the course is tailor-made for them, rather than something taken off the shelf each time it might be needed.

Production of Materials

Design

Your course documentation should reflect the care you take to design and deliver an effective training event. It is therefore worth spending time on the design and lay-out of your material

Dense blocks of text are uninviting and difficult to read, so break them up into short paragraphs with headings and bullet points. If you have got access to a desk-top publishing system or sophisticated word processor, then you will be able to add rules, boxes, tints and various other features that will enhance the effect.

Good Training Practice

Interactive handouts, self-assessment forms, etc. are all designed to help course members to be active participants in the learning process, but they will do this only if participants know why you are using them and if you use them consistently. For example, using the self-assessment forms for one activity and forgetting to use it for another, suggests that self-assessment isn't important.

You will probably have invested a lot of time in preparing your documentation, so you will want to ensure that its use justifies this investment. If you spend some time working through the material rather than just handing it out, participants are more likely to value your efforts.

10 Simulation and Simulators

▷   SUMMARY   ◁

This chapter:
- Discusses the use of simulation and simulators as training aids.
- Gives examples of different types with particular reference to computer-based simulation.
- Describes the range of computer hardware available for running simulation software.
- Suggests some ways of using computer-based training and standard computer applications on training courses.

Before plunging into the nitty-gritty aspects of simulation and simulators in the context of training aids, some rather abstract information is necessary for clarification.

Background information

Simulation in training is a dynamic representation of a real process or task. Does this tell you anything? Perhaps it will if we unravel it.

The dynamic aspect means that the situation evolves according to what the participants do. They therefore see the cumulative consequences of their decisions. The element of reality means that the simulation is not controlled by an arbitrary set of rules, nor is it necessarily competitive (unless competition is a necessary feature of the real thing).

The representation of reality (i.e. the 'fidelity' of the simulation) has two dimensions:

- the external, physical conditions (the equipment, the noise, the time constraints, the surroundings etc.)
- the internal, psychological conditions (the personal feelings involved, the amount of stress felt, the extent to which participants need to feel engaged).

The degree of fidelity that you need in a simulation in each of these dimensions will depend on:

- the nature and complexity of the task
- the level of skill and experience that the trainees have
- your training objectives.

Simulation is used when learning in the real situation would be too:

- dangerous
- expensive
- inconvenient
- time consuming.

The simulator is the equipment used to create the appropriate conditions for a simulation.

This is the background information you need; a few examples will bring it to life.

Examples of Simulation and Simulators

A computerised flight simulator provides such a high degree of fidelity that the experience of 'flying' is virtually indistinguishable from being in a real aircraft. It provides the opportunity for pilots, usually at an advanced stage of their training, to practise complex and potentially dangerous procedures and manoeuvres with no risk to themselves or to the aircraft.

Civil airlines use 'evacuation trainers' to train cabin staff in emergency procedures. The simulator is an exact replication of the passenger cabin part of the aircraft, and it recreates conditions such as fire, smoke, jammed doors and tilted floors. Staff respond as they would in a real crisis, by opening the emergency exits and sliding out down the evacuation chutes.

Both the above examples recreate reality to an unnerving degree, because they are dealing with life and death situations. Without this fidelity, their effectiveness in training would be reduced.

However, simulators are not restricted to large, high-tech, expensive recreations of the real thing. At the opposite end of the spectrum there are numerous ingenious low-tech examples, including a calving simulator consisting of elastic luggage straps and shaped PVC sleeves filled with water! In this case, there is only a limited reproduction of the real situation, to allow users to concentrate on some basic skills.

In the less exotic world of management and business simulations, the focus is on developing cognitive and behavioural skills. Instead of being based on a simulator – i.e. a piece of equipment with certain characteristics that more or less represents the real thing – they use a range of materials, and sometimes none at all.

An example of simulation at its simplest form would be role-playing. For the simulation of many situations in which behavioural skills are important, there is no need to represent the physical context in which they would be used. It is often irrelevant whether the background is an office, a production line, a retail outlet or a warehouse. It is the interaction between people that has to be simulated, so the psychological dimension of reality is the important one. The more participants are aware of the nature of the situation they are recreating – the feelings it can engender, the directions it could take and the way it could affect people – the more they will be able to create a realistic situation in which to practise their skills.

One step along the physical dimension of reality takes you to the management 'in-tray' exercises, which simulate the judgements and decision making that characterize managerial jobs. The resources are paper based materials in the form of memos, reports, letters and other sorts of written information that cross the manager's desk. In its simplest form, the only other aspect of reality that is introduced is a time restriction. For a greater degree of realism, the individual will be interrupted by telephone calls or people 'dropping in' from time to time, and will be given new information that has to be integrated with what was in the original in-tray.

Greater complexity can be featured in business simulations. Some use computers to manipulate data according to the decisions entered by individuals or groups taking part. In the course of a few hours, participants might experience and respond to key events that would take months or years in real time.

Since the processing power of computers offers enormous scope for representing reality in so many different ways, it is not surprising that so many recent and current simulations use computers in one form or another. But the purpose of this chapter is not to explore this diverse and potentially powerful training medium for its own sake. Instead, it will be emphasizing how you can make use of computer-based simulation as a training aid in a conventional training situation.

Computer-based Simulation

Description of the Equipment

The rapid development of the microcomputer in terms of speed and processing power has meant that quite sophisticated simulations can be produced and run on desk-top computers that are found in any office or training department. The IBM PC and its compatibles are the most common machines, but the Apple Macintosh, the Atari ST, the Commodore Amiga and the Acorn Archimedes can also be found in many organizations and educational establishments. The modern versions of these machines are capable of producing the high quality colour graphics usually needed for convincing simulations and they can all run programs that are controlled by a mouse, which makes life simple for users as it cuts the amount of typing they have to do.

A mouse is a small hand operated device that is moved around on the desk-top. As it moves, a pointer on the screen mimics the action and allows commands to be sent to the computer by clicking on a menu item rather than typing them in.

This book cannot possibly explain in detail the workings of computers, but it will give a very brief outline of the things you will need to look out for.

If there is no one in your department or organization who can demystify these aspects of computers, and you need help, a good supplier will be able to explain what would best suit your needs – but get several opinions.

The IBM PC and Compatibles

Since its early days as a desk-top or personal computer, the IBM PC has developed from a humble machine that was designed to compete with the early home/business computers, into a fast and sophisticated business machine with a confusing array of models and plug in cards.

The basic model – the IBM PC – has been replaced with several upgraded models called ISA (Industry Standard Architecture) machines such as the IBM AT and more recently by the MCA (Microchannel Architecture) machines such as the PS/2. All the machines can be modified or customized by using plug-in cards, and this is where much of the confusion arises. If you've glanced through any computer magazine, you will have come across terms such as EGA, VGA, super VGA, Hi-res colour graphics and many more.

EGA stands for 'enhanced graphics adaptor' and will allow the display of 16 colours simultaneously at a resolution of 640 × 350 pixels (picture elements). VGA stands for video graphic array that will display 256 colours simultaneously at a resolution of 320 × 200 pixels, or 16 colours simultaneously at a maximum resolution of 640 × 480 pixels. These and other common display modes are shown in Figure 10.1.

Display adaptor	Feature			
	Mono	Colour	No. colours on screen	Resolution (pixels)
CGA	Y	Y	2	640 x 200
			4	320 x 200
Hercules	Y	N	2	720 x 348
EGA	Y	Y	16	640 x 200
			16	640 x 350
VGA	Y	Y	16	640 x 480
			256	320 x 200
Extended VGA	Y	Y	16	1024 x 768
			256	640 x 480

Figure 10.1 *Features of some common display modes on the IBM PC and compatible computers*

For use in a training context, the most important feature of the computer will probably be the facility to display good quality colour graphics. So you will need a model that has at least an EGA or preferably a VGA colour graphics card, and a colour monitor. You will also need a hard disk drive with at least 30 megabytes of storage, and a mouse.

The other main specifications you are likely to come across relate to the amount of main memory or RAM (random access memory), the type and speed of the microprocessor installed, and the number and types of disk drive fitted. Most modern machines will have a memory of at least 640 kilobytes, which should be sufficient for running most software applications, but the size of memory continues to be increased so that 1, 2 and 4 megabyte machines are becoming quite common.

The microprocessor types you will see range from the old 8088 to the more modern 80286, 80386 and now the 80486. Their speeds range from 4.77 MHz (megahertz) for the 8088 to more than 30 MHz for the 80486. The main differences between these microprocessors lies in the speed and power with which they will process information. To trainers, the differences are probably not very important. A more significant feature is likely to be a hard disk drive for storing programs and data.

This will allow you to load and run your software at a much greater speed than if you have to rely on floppy disks. The disk drive is usually built into the machine, and the disks are not accessible to the user. This means that once the software has been transferred to the hard disk from one or more floppy disks, it will remain in the machine (unless it is inadvertently erased). Most machines will also be fitted with at least one and sometimes two floppy disk drives to read floppy disks of either 3.5 inches or 5.25 inches.

The Apple Macintosh

The original Apple Macintosh was fitted with a very small (9 inches) monochrome screen that made it unsuitable for use as a training aid except for the smallest of groups. More recently, Apple have introduced much larger screens and colour monitors that easily rival the top-of-range IBM machines. The main advantages of the Macintosh include the user-friendly graphical interface and the consistently high quality software. Mac software is written to take full advantage of the WIMP (windows, icons, mouse and pull-down menus) environment. The main disadvantages are the price (two or three times the price of a comparable PC) and, from the trainer's point of view, the shortage of computer-based training programs – most are written for the PC.

As with most computer manufacturers, Apple offer a range of models, although this is somewhat smaller than IBM's. The Macintosh II range is likely to be of most interest to the trainer. The main differences within this range are the existence and size of a hard disk (from a machine with only one floppy disk drive to a machine with a floppy disk drive and up to 160 megabyte hard disk), and whether a colour monitor is supplied or has to be bought as an extra. The colour display of most models in the range is 256 colours at a resolution of 640 × 480 pixels.

Other alternatives

There are many dedicated users of the Atari ST, the Commodore Amiga, and the Acorn Archimedes, especially in education and small businesses, who consider these machines to be economic alternatives to the Apple Macintosh. The Atari and the Commodore are both supplied with a mouse and a WIMP environment; these are optional extras on the Acorn.

The Atari ST is supplied in three main models – the 520STE, the 1040STE and the Mega STE (from 1 to 4 megabytes of memory). There are three screen resolutions available on each model – 640 × 400 pixels monocrome; 640 × 200 pixels with 4 colours; and 320 × 200 pixels with 16 colours from a palette of 4,096. There is also an Atari TT range which is capable of higher resolution graphics – up to 1,280 × 960 pixels monochrome; 640 × 480 pixels with 16 colours; and 320 × 400 with 256 colours in addition to the three ST resolutions. For most serious applications, the 1040STE with 1 megabyte of memory will be a minimum requirement, and the Mega ST with 2 or 4 megabytes the most practical.

In the Commodore series there are two main models – the Amiga A500 with 512 kilobytes of memory and the Amiga A2000 with 1 megabyte. The Amiga has a better colour specification than the Atari ST with a maximum of 32 colours from a palette of 4,096, but in most other respects can be considered as similar.

The Acorn Archimedes is popular in the educational world, partly because of Acorn's foothold that was established with the BBC Micro. The Archimedes is noted for its high resolution colour graphics and its speed of operation due to a microprocessor with a reduced instruction set (RISC). Acorn also produce machines with a much higher specification than the Archimedes, but with a correspondingly higher price tag.

These alternatives to the IBM PC have been mentioned briefly because they may fulfil your needs as a trainer more easily and cheaply. But for many people, the choice will already have been made for them, because the IBM PC has got such a strong hold in so many organizations.

Training Applications

As well as the general justifications for using simulation quoted at the beginning of this chapter, you will have your own reasons for including it in your training. It might be appropriate when:

- real objects, machines or systems are too complicated and inaccessible (as well as possibly too dangerous and expensive) for use as a training aid
- only part of the total task needs to be practised, e.g. applying diagnostic principles in fault-finding, but not actually repairing the equipment
- you want to use an element of guided discovery learning in your training sessions (e.g. 'What will happen if...?') and to show the consequences
- you need a controlled demonstration, which excludes variables that may be irrelevant at a particular stage of training.

With the current power and performance of microcomputers, computer simulation is becoming a more viable option for use on training courses, than would have been the case a few years ago.

Simulations in Computer-based Training (CBT)

Computer-based simulations designed to run on microcomputers are often produced with distance learning in mind, and they will usually be found embedded within a CBT (computer-based training) programme. But, as with interactive video, there is no reason why you as a trainer shouldn't make use of these packages as a resource within a conventional training setting.

EXAMPLE: A FAULT-FINDING SIMULATION

One example, produced by the authors, is a fault finding simulation. Figure 10.2 shows typical screen shots from a CBT program designed for developing fault-finding skills in electricians. Although it was intended for self-study, the simulated faults within the programme can be used as demonstration material within a conventional classroom setting.

In this example the simple electric circuit diagram shows a number of lamps, switches, wires with their various connections and a fuse. The circuit operates just as a real electric circuit would. So when it is working normally you can extinguish the lamps by moving the appropriate switch to OFF, or replace a fuse that has blown, or switch the whole system off at the main switch. You can do this by clicking with the mouse on the appropriate item. This then produces a small menu – in the case of a switch this would simply be an item saying 'Switch OFF?' if the switch was already on. Clicking on the menu item confirms the action and updates the screen to show the result.

Under fault conditions you can conduct tests at any of the terminals, remove wires from any of the terminals, change the fuse and replace any of the main components. You can see the results of these actions by clicking on a menu item and then get more information about what has happened by clicking on the INFO button. A typical message from the INFO

131

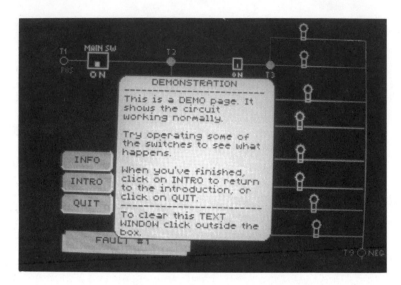

(a)

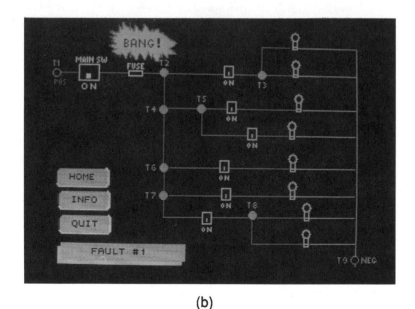

(b)

Figure 10.2 *Typical screens from a CBT programme designed for developing fault-finding skills on electrical circuits*

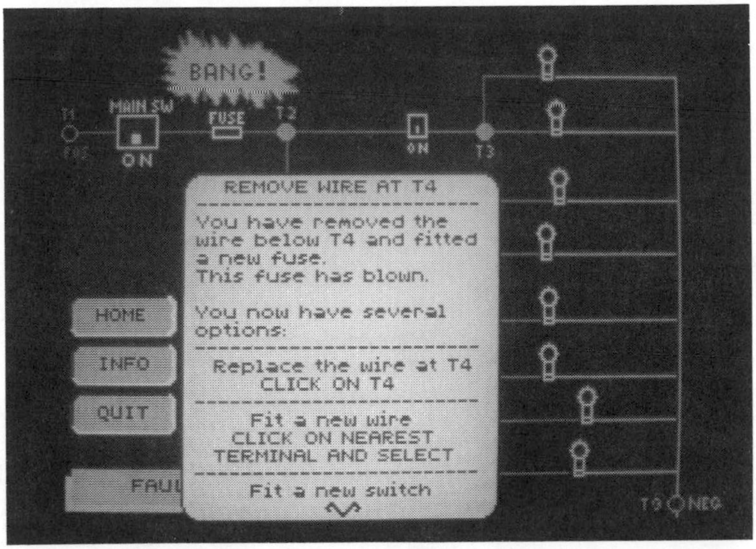

(a)

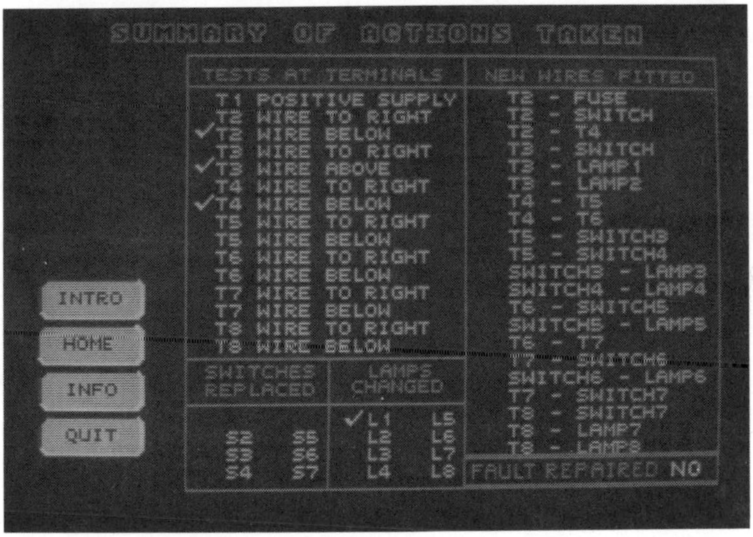

(b)

Figure 10.3 *(a) typical message from the CBT simulation shown in Fig 10.2, accessed by clicking on the INFO button. (b) A summary of actions taken can be accessed at any time from the HOME page*

button is shown in Figure 10.3(a). At any stage you can find out what tests and actions you have already done by clicking on the SUMMARY button on the HOME page. This produces the table shown in Figure 10.3(b).

On a training course the tutor can discuss with a group of trainees what tests at various points in the circuit are likely to show, and then simulate the tests by clicking on any of the 'test' or 'action' choices. After each test or action taken, the CBT program offers some feedback. The tutor can reinforce and add to this feedback as appropriate.

One advantage of using a computer-based simulation in this way, is that the trainees develop a logical and reasoned approach to the subject matter under the personal guidance of a tutor. Part of the tutor's role is to gauge what information and feedback will help individual trainees. In this situation, the computer is being used as a training aid rather than as a self-contained delivery medium.

Many other computer-based simulations are specifically designed to be used under the control of a tutor or instructor. In this 'demonstration' mode, the computer can be used to show the effects of making certain decisions, the relationship between different variables, or the way in which machines or equipment operate under different conditions.

Producing Simulations

One of the main limitations of using simulators in training is that you usually need a specialist company to produce the simulation. Apart from low-tech examples, such as those mentioned above, simulations using a computer can be time consuming to program and usually require the skills of a programmer with a high level of experience in simulation techniques. At least that's what the experts would tell you. If you want a realistic simulation of a complex piece of machinery, with a high level of realism, this may well be true. But there are numerous examples of less ambitious applications that can be produced by using one of the many paint programs, or slide presentation packages, or in the case of business studies, a spreadsheet with a graph drawing facility, such as Lotus 1-2-3. All you need is a little imagination and practice in using the software.

EXAMPLE: USING A SPREADSHEET ON A TRAINING COURSE

A simple example using a spreadsheet is shown in Figure 10.4. The subject is the future value of investments in an annuity and it is taken from a course on finance. The table shown in Figure 10.4(a) was produced by using one of the standard functions in the spreadsheet.

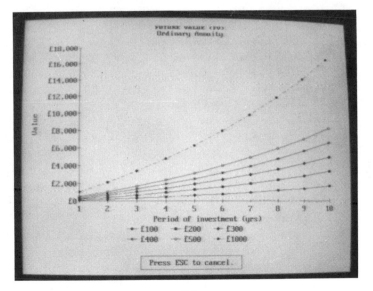

(a)

(b)

Figure 10.4 *A business simulation produced by a computer spreadsheet. (a) A table showing the value of investments over a number of years. (b) The same information shown as a graph can be accessed by selecting an item from the menu bar at the top of the screen*

The figures in the body of the table show the value of the investment after several periods (between one and ten years in this case) for amounts between £100 and £1,000. The interest rate shown at the top of the screen can be altered to any figure and the future value is automatically adjusted to take account of this.

By clicking on a menu item with the mouse, the graph shown in Figure 10.4(b) is displayed. This graph plots the figures from the table and is also automatically updated if the interest rate is changed. In the training session the tutor can demonstrate the effects of changing the interest rate, the amount invested or the period of investment.

The advantage of using the computer compared with using a set of slides is that only the initial spreadsheet needs to be prepared in advance. The variables can be changed according to what is needed during the training session – for example one of the students may suggest a figure and all the tutor has to do is alter the existing entry for that figure and display the result. It is also an easy matter to substitute other financial functions and retain the basic layout of the table and graph or extend it as appropriate.

Authoring languages and hypermedia systems

By using one of the CBT development packages (authoring languages) such as TenCORE or MICROTEXT you can produce simulations that include animation (or pseudo-animation). In fact most CBT programs produced recently have probably used such a language. But these authoring languages generally use a command structure that will take some considerable time to learn, and for most trainers they will not be a feasible means of producing simulations. However, the recent development of hypermedia systems holds out promise for trainers wanting to develop their own material.

Since 1987 Apple have supplied a piece of free software called HyperCard, with all their Macintosh machines. This was designed to produce linked cards of information that could be used in a similar way to CBT screens. The HyperCard system also has facilities to access information from other media such as laser disc players or CD (compact disc) players.

One important idea of the HyperCard system was that teachers or tutors could easily produce learning materials that could be used by their students with a limited knowledge of computing. By clicking on 'buttons' or pre-defined fields with a mouse, the student could move around a connected set of information including text, graphics produced in a paint program, audio from a CD player, or video from a laser disc player. A programming language, HyperTalk, which is contained within HyperCard, can be used to run external programs or routines such as a simulation.

IBM have also produced a hypermedia product called Linkway. Although different in structure and look from HyperCard, Linkway achieves similar results by using pull-down or pop-up menus, and on-screen buttons that are activated by a mouse. It also includes a text editor and paint program so that screens of text and colour images can be created within the programme. Linkway can also access colour images from other programs such as Storyboard, or video sequences from a laser disc player, and there is also a facility for producing animation sequences by linking a series of images from different screens.

As mentioned these hypermedia products are a promising resource for trainers, but there are few examples of their use in the way suggested above. Part of the reason for this may be a lack of knowledge of their existence, and their potential applications. With a little imagination, who knows what you could produce. A revolution in training aids, perhaps?

Further Reading

The following is a selective list of books that expand on some of the training issues that have been discussed briefly.

Barker, John & Tucker, Richard N (1990) *The Interactive Learning Revolution* Nichols Publishing/Kogan Page, London.
A discussion and description of the converging technologies of desk-top publishing, hypermedia and compact disc and their effects on education and training.

Bennett, Roger (Ed.) (1988) *Improving Trainer Effectiveness* Gower Publishing Co Ltd, Aldershot.
A series of contributions from experienced trainers aimed at helping trainers to develop and improve their effectiveness. Many exercises and checklists are included.

Buckley, Roger & Caple, Jim (1990) *The Theory and Practice of Training* Kogan Page, London.
An outline of the issues and concepts of training, dealt with in a systematic way and aimed particularly at the new trainer.

Murphy, Shaun (1990) *A Manager's Guide to Audio-visual Production* Kogan Page, London.
Aimed at managers generally, this guide describes how to produce and use a range of audio-visual aids. The book includes chapters from a number of contributers and a selective index of products and services.

Pont, Tony (1991) *Developing Effective Training Skills* McGraw-Hill, Maidenhead.
A practical guide to designing and running training courses. The book contains chapters on the communication process, audio-visual aids and the evaluation of training, as well as a brief coverage of learning theories and learning methods.

Rae, Leslie (1983) *The Skills of Training* Gower Publishing Co Ltd, Aldershot.
A description of the various approaches to training and training terminology. It is aimed especially at the new trainer, but with sufficient level of detail to be of interest to more experienced training personnel.

Romiszowski, A J (1988) *The Selection and Use of Instructional Media* Kogan Page, London.
An updated edition of Romiszowki's earlier book on the Selection and Use of Teaching Aids. *The wealth of research and theoretical details coupled with practical examples of the media make it a rich source of references for teachers and trainers.*

Sheal, Peter R (1989) *How to Develop and Present Staff Training Courses* Kogan Page, London.
A practical handbook for trainers explaining what is involved in setting up and running a training programme. The book contains numerous diagrams, flowcharts and checklists that can be used as materials for use on courses.

Taylor, Margaret H (1988) *Planning for Video: A Guide to Making Effective Training Videotapes* Nichols Publishing/Kogan Page, London.
A 'how to' book that explains in straightforward steps what needs to go into making a training video. The emphasis is on planning and techniques rather than on using particular types of equipment.

The Training Officer (1982) *Audio Visual Aids in Training* Marylebone Press Ltd, Manchester.
A compact booklet containing a series of articles that were first published in The Training Officer. *The various authors offer plenty of useful tips in preparing and presenting information via the OHP, film, tape and video.*

Useful Addresses

Listed below are addresses of suppliers of products mentioned in this book, together with other major suppliers of training videos.

Videos

Association of Professional Video Distributors
P O Box 25, Godalming, Surrey, UK GU7 1PL. Tel. 04868 23429.

BBC Enterprises
UK – BBC Training Videos, Woodlands, 80 Wood Lane, London W12 0TT. Tel. 081 576 2361.
Canada – BBC Training Videos, Cinevillage, 65 Heward Avenue, Suite 111, Toronto, Ontario M4M 2T5. Tel. 416 469 1505
USA – BBC Lionheart, 630 5th Avenue, Suite 2220, New York 10111. Tel. 212 373 4000.

Longman Training
UK – Longman House, Burnt Hill, Harlow, Essex CM20 2JE. Tel. 0279 426721
USA – CRM Films, 2233 Faraday Avenue, Carlsbad, California 92008. Tel. 619 431 9800.

Melrose Film Productions Limited
UK – 16 Bromells Road, London SW4 0BL. Tel. 071-627 8404.
USA – Video Learning, 354 West Lancaster Avenue, Suite 105, Haverford, Pennsylvania 19041. Tel. 215 896 6600.

Video Arts Limited
UK – Dumbarton House, 68 Oxford Street, London W1N 9LA. Tel. 071-637 7288.

USA – Video Arts Inc., Northbrook Tech Center, 4088 Commercial Avenue, Northbrook, Illinois 60062. Tel. 708 291 1008.

Wyvern Business Training

UK – Wyvern House, 6 The Business Park, Angel Drove, Ely, Cambs CB7 4JW. Tel. 0353 665533.

USA – Telephone Doctor, 12119 St Charles Rock Road, St Louis, Mo 63044. Tel. 314 291 1012; Freephone 800 882 9911.

Other Products

Flipframes are available from:

Don Cresswell Limited, Bridge House, Grange Park, London, UK N21 1BR. Tel. 081-360 6622.

PC Opensoft is available from:

The Soft Option Ltd

Elmtree Road, Teddington, Middlesex, UK TW11 8TD. Tel. 081 977 0272.

The Wolf Visualizer is available from:

TWS plc

185 Walton Summit, Bamberbridge, Preston, Lancs, UK PR5 8AJ Tel. 0772 37249 or

Wolf audio-visuals GmbH,

Vorarlberger Wirtschaftspark, A-6840 Gotzis, Austria. Tel. +43-5523/52250-0.

Index